Step Forward

Language for Everyday Life

SERIES DIRECTOR
Jayme Adelson-Goldstein

Includes
Student Audio CD

1

Jane Spigarelli

OXFORD
UNIVERSITY PRESS

OXFORD
UNIVERSITY PRESS

198 Madison Avenue
New York, NY 10016 USA

Great Clarendon Street, Oxford OX2 6DP UK

Oxford University Press is a department of the University of Oxford.
It furthers the University's objective of excellence in research, scholarship,
and education by publishing worldwide in

Oxford New York

Auckland Cape Town Dar es Salaam Hong Kong Karachi
Kuala Lumpur Madrid Melbourne Mexico City Nairobi
New Delhi Shanghai Taipei Toronto

With offices in

Argentina Austria Brazil Chile Czech Republic France Greece
Guatemala Hungary Italy Japan Poland Portugal Singapore
South Korea Switzerland Thailand Turkey Ukraine Vietnam

OXFORD and OXFORD ENGLISH are registered trademarks of
Oxford University Press

© Oxford University Press 2008

Database right Oxford University Press (maker)

Library of Congress Cataloging-in-Publication Data
Step Forward : English for everyday life.
    p. cm.
  Step Forward 1 by Jane Spigarelli; Step Forward 2 by Ingrid Wisniewska.
  ISBN: 978-0-19-439224-2 (1 : pbk.)
  ISBN: 978-0-19-439225-9 (2 : pbk.)
  1. English language—Textbooks for foreign students. 2. English language–
Problems, exercises, etc. I. Spigarelli, Jane. II. Wisniewska, Ingrid.
  PE1128.S2143 2006
  428.2'4—dc22
                          2006040090

Executive Publisher: Janet Aitchison
Editorial Manager: Stephanie Karras
Editors: Margaret Brooks, Glenn Mathes II, Sharon Sargent
Associate Editor: Olga Christopoulos
Art Director: Maj-Britt Hagsted
Senior Designer: Claudia Carlson
Senior Art Editor: Judi DeSouter
Art Editor: Elizabeth Blomster
Manufacturing Manager: Shanta Persaud
Manufacturing Coordinator: Faye Wang

Student Book ISBN: 978 0 19 439224 2
Student Book with CD-ROM ISBN: 978 0 19 439653 0
Student Book as pack component ISBN: 978 0 19 439658 5
Audio CD-ROM as pack component ISBN: 978 0 19 439663 9

Printed in Hong Kong
10 9 8 7 6 5 4 3 2 1

The publishers would like to thank the following for their permission to adapt
copyright material:
p. 72 "Americans Spending More Time on Themselves, Says NPD Study" used
with permission of The NPD Group
p. 144 "General Facts" used with permission of www.greetingcard.org

ACKNOWLEDGMENTS

Cover photograph: Corbis/Punchstock
Back cover photograph: Brian Rose

Illustrations by: Silke Bachmann, p.6 (man and woman), p.43 (kitchen), p.47, p.71
(supermarket), p.114, 118; Barb Bastian, p.17, p.52; Ken Batelman, p.53, p.56, p.97,
p.109, p.128; John Batten, p.43 (two women), p.48 (top illus.), p.68, p.83 (clothes),
p.104, p.130 (split screen); Annie Bissett, p.24, p.58 (map bottom), p.73, p.145; Dan
Brown, p.5, p.101; Claudia Carlson, p.173 (map); Gary Ciccarelli, p.2 (top and bottom
illus.), p.112; Sam and Amy Collins, p.100; Laurie Conley, p.113; Lyndall Culbertson,
p.61, p.148, p.152, p.155, p.158, p.159; Jeff Fillbach, p.12, p.31, p.34 (phone
conversation), p.70 (cartoon); Debby Fisher, p.4, p.16, p.64 (activities); Martha Gavin,
p.30, p.54, p.66, p.78, p.90; Paul Hampson, p.32, p.80, p.106, p.127, p.139 (cartoon);
Mark Hannon, p.9, p.18, p.79, p.102, p.116, p.126, p.130 (911 emergencies), p.138;
Michael Hortens, p.19, p.48 (article), p.49; Rod Hunt, p.40, p.41; Jon Keegan, p.46
(note), p.77, p.108 (OTC medicine); Uldis Klavins, p.124, p.125; Shelton Leong, p.10
(conversation), p.22 (realia), p.35, p.42, p.58, p.60 (home emergencies), p.72, p.82
(two women), p.94 (cartoon), p.103, p.140; Scott MacNeill, p.8, p.38, p.54 (locations),
p.60 (poster), p.82 (realia), p.91, p.132 (car), p.144; Kevin McCain, p.137; Karen Minot,
p.28 (family album), p.34 (calendar), p.46 (utility bills), p.59, p.83 (receipt), p.94
(menu), p.95, p.121, p.139, p.142; Derek Mueller, p.89; Tom Newsom, p.65, p.88;
Terry Paczko, p.3 (numbers and addresses), p.70 (office actions), p.71 (office actions),
p.76, p.84; Geo Parkin, p.136; Roger Penwill, p.10 (cartoon), p.15, p.27, p.44, p.51,
p.63, p.75, p.87, p.99, p.111, p.123, p.135, p.147; Karen Prichett, p.28 (people), p.29.

We would like to thank the following for their permission to reproduce photographs:

Alamy: oote boe, p.13 (money exchange); Banana Stock, p.19 (Asian female), p.22
(Indian female); Bluestone Prod., p.67 (grocery clerk); Rolf Bruderer, p.20 (laughing
man); Comstock, p.108 (doctor and patient); Dennis Kitchen Studions, p.15
(students); Design Pics, Inc., p.13 (flag); Dynamic Graphics, p.13 (doctor); Justine Eun
for OUP, p.44 (women eating lunch); Fogstock, LLC, p.13 (construction worker); Getty
Images: Photodisc, p.134 (road work sign); Michael Goldman, p.39 (Hispanic male);
Henry Westhein Photography, p.22 (Chinese wedding couple); IndexOpen: Ablestock,
p.12 (adult students); Inmagine: Creatas, p.12 (woman reading), p.13 (teacher
and student), p.36 (large family), p.134 (children crossing sign); Jupiter Images:
Comstock, p.12 (two women talking); Kim Karapeles, p.134 (no parking sign);
Masterfile: Dana Hursey, p.13 (men talking); Ryoko Mathes, p.20 (angry man); Medio
Images, p.108 (man running); MIXA Co., Ltd., p.36 (mother and adult children);
Omni Photo, p.20 (hungry dog); Photodisc, p.19 (Asian senior); Photo Edit Inc.:
Michelle D. Bridwell, p.127 (anchorwoman); Punchstock: Corbis, p.20 (tired man),
44 (window washing); Purestock, p.108 (woman eating apple); Anthony Redpath,
p.19 (Hispanic female); Bryan Reinhart, p.20 (graduate and parents); Shelley Rotner,
p.130 (ambulance); Royalty Free Division, p.115 (reading newspaper); Rubberball
Productions, p.22 (African male); David Schmidt, p.19 (Asian male); Stockbyte, p.12
(student on campus); SuperStock: Powerstock, p.120 (time clock); SuperStock: Powerstock, p.20 (worried
mother); Thinkstock, p.36 (small family); Transparencies, Inc., p.134 (speed limit
sign); Scott Tysick, p.44 (woman cleaning); Jim Whitmers, p.7 (Hispanic male).

We are grateful for the commitment, talent, and collaborative
spirit of the *Step Forward Book 1* editorial and design team:
Stephanie Karras, Meg Brooks, Sharon Sargent, Amy Cooper,
Glenn Mathes, Carla Mavrodin, Maj-Britt Hagsted,
Claudia Carlson, and Lissy Blomster.
We also thank our students and colleagues for their many
insights and boundless inspiration.

Jane Spigarelli
Jayme Adelson-Goldstein

I would like to thank Jayme Adelson-Goldstein for her wit,
wisdom, and generosity along the way.
This book is for my husband, Chris Monte, whose infinite
support makes all things possible.

–Jane

I thank Jane Spigarelli for bringing her many gifts to this
book, including her unique blend of imaginative and
practical thinking. This book is for James, Leo, Lila,
Victoria, and Kathryn.

–Jayme

ACKNOWLEDGMENTS

The Publisher and Series Director would like to acknowledge the following individuals for their invaluable input during the development of this series:

Vittoria Abbatte-Maghsoudi Mount Diablo Unified School District, Loma Vista Adult Center, Concord, CA

Karen Abell Durham Technical Community College, Durham, NC

Millicent Alexander Los Angeles Unified School District, Huntington Park-Bell Community Adult School, Los Angeles, CA

Diana Allen Oakton Community College, Skokie, IL

Bethany Bandera Arlington Education and Employment Program, Arlington, VA

Sandra Bergman New York City Department of Education, New York, NY

Chan Bostwick Los Angeles Technology Center, Los Angeles, CA

Diana Brady-Herndon Napa Valley Adult School, Napa, CA

Susen Broellos Baldwin Park Unified School District, Baldwin Park, CA

Carmen Carbajal Mitchell Community College, Statesville, NC

Jose Carmona Daytona Beach Community College, Daytona Beach, FL

Ingrid Caswell Los Angeles Technology Center, Los Angeles, CA

Joyce Clapp Hayward Adult School, Hayward, CA

Beverly deNicola Capistrano Unified School District, San Juan Capistrano, CA

Edward Ende Miami Springs Adult Center, Miami Springs, FL

Gayle Fagan Harris County Department of Education, Houston, TX

Richard Firsten Lindsey Hopkins Technical Education Center, Miami, FL

Elizabeth Fitzgerald Hialeah Adult Center, Hialeah, FL

Mary Ann Florez Arlington Education and Employment Program, Arlington, VA

Leslie Foster Davidson Mitchell Community College, Statesville, NC

Beverly Gandall Santa Ana College School of Continuing Education, Santa Ana, CA

Rodriguez Garner Westchester Community College, Valhalla, NY

Sally Gearhart Santa Rosa Junior College, Santa Rosa, CA

Norma Guzman Baldwin Park Unified School District, Baldwin Park, CA

Lori Howard UC Berkeley, Education Extension, Berkeley, CA

Phillip L. Johnson Santa Ana College Centennial Education Center, Santa Ana, CA

Kelley Keith Mount Diablo Unified School District, Loma Vista Adult Center, Concord, CA

Blanche Kellawon Bronx Community College, Bronx, NY

Keiko Kimura Triton College, River Grove, IL

Jody Kirkwood ABC Adult School, Cerritos, CA

Matthew Kogan Evans Community Adult School, Los Angeles, CA

Laurel Leonard Napa Valley Adult School, Napa, CA

Barbara Linek Illinois Migrant Education Council, Plainfield, IL

Alice Macondray Neighborhood Centers Adult School, Oakland, CA

Ronna Magy Los Angeles Unified School District Central Office, Los Angeles, CA

Jose Marlasca South Area Adult Education, Melbourne, FL

Laura Martin Adult Learning Resource Center, Des Plaines, IL

Judith Martin-Hall Indian River Community College, Fort Pierce, FL

Michael Mason Mount Diablo Unified School District, Loma Vista Adult Center, Concord, CA

Katherine McCaffery Brewster Technical Center, Tampa, FL

Cathleen McCargo Arlington Education and Employment Program, Arlington, VA

Todd McDonald Hillsborough County Public Schools, Tampa, FL

Rita McSorley Northeast Independent School District, San Antonio, TX

Gloria Melendrez Evans Community Adult School, Los Angeles, CA

Vicki Moore El Monte-Rosemead Adult School, El Monte, CA

Meg Morris Mountain View Los Altos Adult Education District, Los Altos, CA

Nieves Novoa LaGuardia Community College, Long Island City, NY

Jo Pamment Haslett Public Schools, East Lansing, MI

Liliana Quijada-Black Irvington Learning Center, Houston, TX

Ellen Quish LaGuardia Community College, Long Island City, NY

Mary Ray Fairfax County Public Schools, Springfield, VA

Tatiana Roganova Hayward Adult School, Hayward, CA

Nancy Rogensky-Roda Hialeah-Miami Lakes Adult Education and Community Center, Hialeah, FL

Lorraine Romero Houston Community College, Houston, TX

Edilyn Samways The English Center, Miami, FL

Kathy Santopietro Weddel Northern Colorado Literacy Program, Littleton, CO

Dr. G. Santos The English Center, Miami, FL

Fran Schnall City College of New York Literacy Program, New York, NY

Mary Segovia El Monte-Rosemead Adult School, El Monte, CA

Edith Smith City College of San Francisco, San Francisco, CA

Alisa Takeuchi Chapman Education Center, Garden Grove, CA

Leslie Weaver Fairfax County Public Schools, Falls Church, VA

David Wexler Napa Valley Adult School, Napa, CA

Bartley P. Wilson Northeast Independent School District, San Antonio, TX

Emily Wonson Hunter College, New York, NY

TABLE OF CONTENTS

Unit	Life Skills & Civics Competencies	Vocabulary	Grammar	Critical Thinking & Math Concepts	Reading & Writing
Pre-unit **The First Step** **page 2**	• Respond to basic classroom directions • Say and spell names • Identify and read numbers, phone numbers, and addresses	• Names • Numbers	• Imperatives	• Read, write, and identify numbers 1–100 • Identify and read phone numbers	• Write names • Read and write numbers 1–100
Unit 1 **In the Classroom** **page 4**	• Give and respond to classroom directions • Identify classroom items • Respond to simple commands • Read and complete school forms • Give personal information • Begin and end social conversations • State personal goals	• Classroom directions • Classroom items • Items on a form • Social conversations	• Singular and plural forms • Statements with *be* • Subject pronouns • Contractions with *be* • *Who* and *What*	• Differentiate between: elements of personal information; telling, spelling, printing, and signing; phone numbers, zip codes, and other numbers • Identify effective language-learning habits • Analyze personal language-learning goals **Problem solving:** • Respond appropriately to greetings and introductions	• Read and complete school forms • Write personal information • Read a school poster • Write sentences using contractions • Write sentences about the classroom
Unit 2 **My Classmates** **page 16**	• Interpret clock times • Identify days, months, years, and dates • Read a calendar • Identify colors • Ask and answer personal information questions • Complete an extended form • Interpret population data	• Times • Days, months, years, and dates • Colors • Items on a form • Feelings • Marital titles • Population and immigration terms	• Information questions with *be* • *Yes/No* questions with *be*	• Interpret clock times and dates • Interpret a calendar • Analyze population statistics • Interpret graphs **Real-life math:** • Synthesize information to create a graph **Problem solving:** • Determine how to solve problems and ask for help in the classroom	• Read and write about a calendar • Read ID cards • Read about feelings • Write answers to *Yes/No* questions • Read an article about U.S. population and immigration statistics • Write sentences about a graph
Unit 3 **Family and Friends** **page 28**	• Identify family members • State hair and eye color • Describe people • Take a phone message • Ask for and give dates • Talk about birthdays	• Family members • Eye color • Hair color • Other physical descriptions • Ordinal numbers • Percentages	• *A* or *an* • Possessives • Questions and answers with possessives	• Identify dates • Recognize and associate ordinal numbers with dates • Compare family sizes • Interpret information in a chart • Recognize percentages **Real-life math:** • Calculate days between events **Problem solving:** • Find and correct an error on a document	• Read dates • Read about a family • Write sentences about physical descriptions • Write sentences using possessives • Write a phone message • Read an article about family size

Listening & Speaking	CASAS Life Skills Competencies	Standardized Student Syllabi/ LCPs	SCANS Competencies	EFF Content Standards
• Listen to basic classroom directions • Say and spell names • Listen and say numbers, phone numbers, and addresses	0.1.2, 0.1.4, 0.1.6, 6.0.1, 6.0.2	22.01, 25.01	• Listening • Speaking • Sociability	• Speaking so others can understand • Listening actively
• Give classroom directions • Listen for and give personal information • Talk about the classroom • Practice social conversations • Interview a partner to fill out an application **Pronunciation:** • Listen for contractions and use them in conversations	**L1:** 0.1.2, 0.1.5, 7.4.5, 7.4.7 **L2:** 0.1.2, 0.2.1, 0.2.2, 2.5.5, 6.0.1, 7.4.7 **L3:** 0.1.2, 7.4.7 **L4:** 0.1.2, 0.1.4, 0.2.1, 7.4.7 **L5:** 0.1.2, 0.2.2, 2.5.5, 7.4.7 **RE:** 0.1.2, 0.1.4, 0.1.5, 0.2.1, 0.2.2, 4.8.1, 7.2.5–7.2.7, 7.3.1	**L1:** 32.01, 33.06 **L2:** 22.01, 25.01, 31.02, 32.01, 32.02, 32.13 **L3:** 22.01, 32.01, 33.02, 33.06, 33.09 **L4:** 22.01–22.03, 32.01, 32.02, 32.13, 33.09, 34.01, 34.02 **L5:** 22.01, 31.02, 32.01, 32.03, 32.04, 32.13 **RE:** 22.01–22.03, 32.01, 32.02, 32.05, 32.13, 33.02, 33.06, 33.07, 33.09	Most SCANS are incorporated into this unit, with an emphasis on: • Seeing things in the mind's eye • Self-management • Participating as a member of a team	Most EFFs are incorporated into this unit, with an emphasis on: • Observing critically • Cooperating with others • Reflecting and evaluating • Solving problems and making decisions
• Ask and answer questions with time and calendar words • Talk about a calendar • Listen for information about people • Listen for information about ID cards • Ask and answer personal information questions • Listen for information on an extended form	**L1:** 0.1.2, 2.3.1, 2.3.2, 6.0.1, 7.1.4, 7.4.5, 7.4.7 **L2:** 0.1.2, 0.1.4, 0.2.1, 6.01, 7.4.7 **L3:** 0.1.1, 0.1.2, 0.2.1, 7.4.7 **L4:** 0.1.2, 0.1.3, 0.2.1, 0.2.2, 6.0.1, 7.4.7 **L5:** 0.1.2, 0.2.1, 1.1.3, 2.7.2, 5.2.4, 5.2.5, 5.5.1, 6.0.1, 6.7.1, 6.7.2, 6.9.2 **RE:** 0.1.2, 0.1.5, 0.2.1, 2.3.2, 4.8.1, 6.0.1, 7.2.5–7.2.7, 7.3.1	**L1:** 25.01–25.03, 32.01, 33.07 **L2:** 22.01, 22.02, 25.01, 25.04, 32.01, 32.02, 32.13, 33.07 **L3:** 22.01, 32.01, 33.02 **L4:** 22.01, 22.03, 25.01, 32.01, 32.02, 33.02, 33.07 **L5:** 22.01, 25.01, 32.01, 32.02–32.05, 32.06, 32.13 **RE:** 22.01, 25.01, 25.03, 32.01, 32.13, 33.02, 33.07	Most SCANS are incorporated into this unit, with an emphasis on: • Seeing things in the mind's eye • Self-management • Acquiring and evaluating information • Interpreting and communicating information	Most EFFs are incorporated into this unit, with an emphasis on: • Observing critically • Using math to solve problems and communicate • Cooperating with others
• Listen for and talk about physical descriptions • Listen to phone messages • Talk about names and birthdays **Pronunciation:** • Ordinal numbers	**L1:** 0.1.2, 7.4.5, 7.4.7 **L2:** 0.1.2, 0.2.1, 7.4.7 **L3:** 0.1.2, 0.2.1, 7.4.7 **L4:** 0.1.2, 2.1.7, 2.3.2, 6.0.1, 6.0.2, 7.4.7 **L5:** 0.1.2, 0.2.1, 6.0.1, 6.0.2, 6.4.2, 6.7.4 **RE:** 0.1.2, 0.2.1, 4.8.1, 6.0.1, 7.2.5–7.2.7, 7.3.1, 7.3.2, 7.3.3, 7.3.4	**L1:** 22.01, 25.03, 31.01, 32.01, 32.02, 33.05 **L2:** 22.01, 31.01, 32.01, 32.02, 33.03 **L3:** 22.01, 31.01, 32.01, 32.13, 33.03, 33.07 **L4:** 22.03, 23.02, 25.01, 25.03, 31.01, 32.01, 32.02, 32.13, 34.01, 34.02 **L5:** 22.01, 25.01, 31.01, 32.01, 32.03–32.06, 33.03 **RE:** 22.01, 25.01, 25.03, 25.04, 31.01, 32.01, 32.02, 32.05, 33.02, 33.03, 33.05, 33.07	Most SCANS are incorporated into this unit, with an emphasis on: • Seeing things in the mind's eye • Self-management • Acquiring and evaluating information • Participating as a member of a team • Organizing and maintaining information	Most EFFs are incorporated into this unit, with an emphasis on: • Observing critically • Using math to solve problems and communicate • Cooperating with others • Solving problems and making decisions • Reflecting and evaluating

Unit	Life Skills & Civics Competencies	Vocabulary	Grammar	Critical Thinking & Math Concepts	Reading & Writing
Unit 4 **At Home** **page 40**	• Identify colors • Identify places and things in the home • State the location of things in the home • State common activities in the home • Ask a friend for help • Save money by conserving resources • Pay bills and address envelopes	• Rooms and other areas in the home • Furniture and appliances • Things to do at home • Items on a bill • Items on an envelope	• *This* and *that* • The present continuous • Present continuous *Yes/No* questions • Subject and object pronouns	• Describe objects in rooms • Analyze personal activity times • Decide when to pay bills **Real-life math:** • Add utility bill totals **Problem solving:** • Delegate responsibility	• Read about a day at home • Write a story about places and activities at home • Read about things to do in the home • Read about paying bills • Read about saving money • Read addresses on envelopes • Write about objects in rooms
Unit 5 **In the Neighborhood** **page 52**	• Identify neighborhood places and modes of transportation • Read a neighborhood map • Ask for and give directions • Respond to emergencies • Use an emergency exit map	• Places in a neighborhood • Things in a neighborhood • Descriptions of locations • Directions • Emergencies	• Prepositions of location • *There is* and *There are* • Questions and answers with *There is* and *There are* • *How many*	• Interpret information from a map • Label a map • Ask for and give directions • Make an emergency exit map **Real-life math:** • Determine distance between points on a map **Problem solving:** • Determine what to do when lost	• Read and write about a neighborhood • Write questions with *Is there* and *Are there* • Write a list of home emergencies • Read about home emergencies • Read emergency exit maps
Unit 6 **Daily Routines** **page 64**	• Identify and discuss daily routines • Make a schedule • State ways to relax • Follow directions to operate office machines • Interpret personal, family, and work responsibilities	• Everyday activities • Ways to relax • Office machines and equipment • Housework	• The simple present • Contractions of *do* • Questions and answers using the simple present • *Have* • *A little* or *a lot*	• Differentiate between daily and special activities • Analyze problems and ask for help with an office machine • Estimate duration of various activities **Problem solving:** • Determine how to solve problems and ask for help in the workplace	• Read and write about a work schedule • Read about office machines and equipment • Read and write about daily routines in the U.S.

Listening & Speaking	CASAS Life Skills Competencies	Standardized Student Syllabi/ LCPs	SCANS Competencies	EFF Content Standards
• Talk about objects in the home • Listen for appliances and furniture • Talk about paying bills • Listen for bill totals • Talk about activities done in the home	**L1:** 0.1.2, 1.4.1, 7.4.5 **L2:** 0.1.2, 1.4.1, 7.4.7, 8.2.5 **L3:** 0.1.2, 0.2.4, 7.4.7, 8.2.3 **L4:** 0.1.2, 0.1.3, 0.2.3, 1.2.4, 1.5.3, 2.1.4, 6.0.1–6.0.4, 6.1.1, 7.1.3, 7.4.7 **L5:** 0.1.2, 1.5.3, 2.1.4, 2.4.1, 6.0.1, 7.1.3 **RE:** 0.1.2, 1.4.1, 4.8.1, 7.2.5–7.2.7, 7.3.1	**L1:** 32.01, 33.03 **L2:** 32.01, 32.02, 32.13, 33.03 **L3:** 32.01, 33.02, 33.07 **L4:** 22.03, 23.03, 25.01, 28.05, 29.01, 32.01, 32.02, 33.01 **L5:** 23.03, 25.01, 28.05, 29.01, 32.01–32.04, 32.12, 32.13 **RE:** 28.05, 32.01, 32.02, 32.05, 32.13, 33.01, 33.02	Most SCANS are incorporated into this unit, with an emphasis on: • Seeing things in the mind's eye • Self-management • Participating as a member of a team	Most EFFs are incorporated into this unit, with an emphasis on: • Observing critically • Cooperating with others • Using math to solve problems and communicate • Solving problems and making decisions
• Talk about transportation and places • Listen for places and things on a map • Listen for neighborhood information • Ask and answer questions with *There is* and *There are* • Listen for and give directions **Pronunciation:** • Stressed words in descriptions	**L1:** 0.1.2, 1.1.3, 2.2.1, 2.2.3, 2.2.5, 2.5.1, 2.5.3, 2.5.5, 7.4.5, 7.4.7 **L2:** 0.1.2, 1.1.3, 2.2.1, 2.5.1, 2.5.3, 7.4.7 **L3:** 0.1.2, 2.2.1, 2.6.1, 6.0.1, 7.4.7 **L4:** 0.1.2, 0.1.3, 1.1.3, 1.1.4, 1.9.4, 2.2.1, 6.0.1, 7.4.7 **L5:** 0.1.2, 1.1.3, 1.4.8, 2.1.2, 2.5.1 **RE:** 0.1.2, 4.8.1, 7.2.5–7.2.7, 7.3.1	**L1:** 26.01, 26.03, 32.01, 32.13 **L2:** 26.03, 32.01, 32.02, 32.13, 33.04 **L3:** 26.03, 32.01, 32.05, 32.13 **L4:** 22.03, 25.01, 26.03, 30.02, 32.01, 32.02, 34.02 **L5:** 26.03, 27.01, 32.01–32.04, 32.06, 32.16 **RE:** 26.03, 32.01, 32.02, 32.05, 33.04	Most SCANS are incorporated into this unit, with an emphasis on: • Seeing things in the mind's eye • Self-management • Participating as a member of a team • Acquiring and evaluating information • Interpreting and communicating information	Most EFFs are incorporated into this unit, with an emphasis on: • Observing critically • Cooperating with others • Using math to solve problems and communicate • Reflecting and evaluating
• Talk about daily routines • Talk about times for daily routines • Listen for information about a work schedule • Talk about a work schedule • Ask and answer questions about daily routines **Pronunciation:** • Verbs ending in *-s*	**L1:** 0.1.2, 0.2.4, 6.0.1, 7.4.5, 7.4.7 **L2:** 0.1.2, 0.2.4, 6.0.1, 7.4.7, 8.2.3 **L3:** 0.1.2, 0.2.4, 3.5.4, 3.5.5, 6.0.1, 7.4.7, 8.1.1 **L4:** 0.1.2, 0.1.3, 0.2.4, 1.7.3, 4.5.1, 4.5.4, 4.5.7, 4.6.1 **L5:** 0.1.2, 0.2.4, 1.1.3, 7.2.5, 7.2.6, 8.2.3 **RE:** 0.1.2, 0.2.4, 1.7.3, 4.5.1, 4.5.4, 4.5.7, 4.6.1, 4.8.1, 6.0.1, 7.2.6, 7.2.7, 7.3.1	**L1:** 32.01 **L2:** 32.01, 32.02, 32.13 **L3:** 32.01, 32.13, 33.02 **L4:** 19.02, 21.01, 22.03, 32.01–32.03, 34.01, 34.02, 34.03 **L5:** 32.01, 32.02, 32.04–32.06, 32.13 **RE:** 19.02, 21.01, 32.01, 32.02, 32.05, 32.13, 33.02	Most SCANS are incorporated into this unit, with an emphasis on: • Seeing things in the mind's eye • Self-management • Time • Participating as a member of a team • Acquiring and evaluating information • Interpreting and communicating information	Most EFFs are incorporated into this unit, with an emphasis on: • Observing critically • Using math to solve problems and communicate • Cooperating with others

Unit	Life Skills & Civics Competencies	Vocabulary	Grammar	Critical Thinking & Math Concepts	Reading & Writing
Unit 7 **Shop and Spend** **page 76**	• Identify coins, bills, and methods of payment • Inquire about prices of items • Interpret ads • Ask about and describe clothing • Select and buy clothing • Interpret cash register receipts and personal checks • Read how to use an ATM	• Money and methods of payment • Clothing • Shopping • Clothing sizes and prices • ATMs and banking	• *How much/ How many* with the simple present • The simple present with *have, want,* and *need* • Simple present *Yes/ No* questions • *A, some,* and *any*	• Calculate totals of money and personal checks • Examine values of coins and bills • Compare and contrast clothing **Real-life math:** • Calculate amounts of change when paying for items **Problem solving:** • Resolve ATM problems	• Read about shopping at a mall • Write about shopping • Read a clothing ad • Read a cash register receipt • Read about ATMs • Read a personal check • Write clothing descriptions
Unit 8 **Eating Well** **page 88**	• Identify common food and supermarket words • Interpret food ads • Make a shopping list • Interpret a weekly schedule • Interpret a menu • Give and take orders in a restaurant • Interpret food labels	• Food • Food shopping • Ordering food • Nutrition and eating habits	• Frequency expressions • *How often* • Adverbs of frequency	• Interpret items on a menu • Analyze healthy and unhealthy eating habits **Real-life math:** • Calculate the total of a bill **Problem solving:** • Analyze and negotiate good eating habits for family members	• Read and write about food shopping • Read a supermarket ad • Write a shopping list • Read a menu • Read about healthy food • Read food labels • Write questions with *How often*
Unit 9 **Your Health** **page 100**	• Identify parts of the body • Identify illnesses and injuries • Access health-care services • Follow medical instructions and advice • Interpret an appointment card • Make a medical appointment • Read directions and warnings on medicine labels	• Parts of the body • Illness and injury • Medical instructions and advice • Items on an appointment card • Preventive care	• *Have to* • Questions and answers with *have to* • *On* or *at* • Irregular plurals	• Analyze and compare medical advice • Classify obligations by level of importance • Interpret a schedule to make appointments • Interpret warnings on medicine labels **Problem solving:** • Determine how to handle obligations when sick	• Read and write about a doctor's appointment • Write answers to questions using *have to* • Read and complete appointment cards • Read about preventive care • Write about obligations • Read directions and warnings on medicine labels

Listening & Speaking	CASAS Life Skills Competencies	Standardized Student Syllabi/ LCPs	SCANS Competencies	EFF Content Standards
• Listen and talk about currency • Listen and talk about clothing items • Talk about clothing for different occasions • Request specific clothing from a salesperson • Listen for sizes and prices of clothing • Talk about purchases **Pronunciation:** • Differentiate between *-teen* and *-ty* numbers	**L1:** 0.1.2, 1.1.6, 1.2.1, 1.2.4, 1.3.9, 6.0.1–6.0.4, 6.1.1, 7.4.5, 7.4.7 **L2:** 0.1.2, 1.3.1, 1.3.3, 1.3.9, 4.4.1, 6.0.1, 7.4.7 **L3:** 0.1.2, 1.3.9, 7.4.7 **L4:** 0.1.2, 1.1.6, 1.1.9, 1.2.1, 1.2.4, 1.2.5, 1.3.9, 1.6.4, 4.4.1, 6.0.1–6.0.4, 6.1.1, 6.1.2, 7.4.7 **L5:** 0.1.2, 1.1.6, 1.3.1, 1.3.3, 1.8.1, 1.8.2, 6.0.1 **RE:** 0.1.2, 0.1.3, 1.1.6, 1.3.1, 1.3.3, 1.3.9, 1.8.1, 1.8.2, 4.8.1, 4.8.6, 6.0.1–6.0.4, 6.1.2, 7.2.5–7.2.7, 7.3.1	**L1:** 25.01, 25.05, 25.06, 28.02, 32.01, 32.02 **L2:** 28.02, 32.01, 32.02, 32.13 **L3:** 28.02, 32.01, 33.02 **L4:** 25.01, 25.05, 25.06, 28.02, 28.03, 32.01, 32.02, 32.13, 34.01, 34.02, 34.03 **L5:** 25.01, 25.06, 32.01, 32.03–32.07, 32.13 **RE:** 25.01, 25.06, 28.02, 32.01, 32.02, 32.05, 32.13, 33.02	Most SCANS are incorporated into this unit, with an emphasis on: • Seeing things in the mind's eye • Self-management • Participating as a member of a team	Most EFFs are incorporated into this unit, with an emphasis on: • Observing critically • Using math to solve problems and communicate • Cooperating with others • Reflecting and evaluating
• Talk about food shopping • Listen for food items on a shopping list • Talk about routines • Order in a restaurant • Listen for restaurant orders • Talk about food labels **Pronunciation:** • Question and statement intonation patterns	**L1:** 0.1.2, 1.3.8, 7.4.5, 7.4.7 **L2:** 0.1.2, 0.2.4, 1.1.6, 1.2.1, 1.2.5, 1.3.8, 6.0.1, 7.4.7, 8.2.1 **L3:** 0.2.4, 2.3.2, 7.4.7 **L4:** 0.1.2, 0.1.3, 0.1.6, 1.1.6, 1.2.1, 1.2.4, 1.3.8, 2.6.4, 6.0.1–6.0.4, 6.1.1, 7.4.7 **L5:** 0.1.2, 1.3.8, 1.6.1, 3.5.1, 3.5.2 **RE:** 0.2.4, 1.3.8, 4.8.1, 6.0.1, 7.2.5–7.2.7, 7.3.1	**L1:** 28.01, 32.01 **L2:** 28.01, 32.01, 32.02, 32.13 **L3:** 25.03, 32.01, 32.08, 33.08 **L4:** 22.03, 25.01, 28.01, 29.03, 32.01, 32.02, 32.13 **L5:** 27.02, 28.01, 32.01, 32.02–32.06, 32.13 **RE:** 28.01, 31.03, 32.01, 32.02, 32.05, 32.13, 33.08	Most SCANS are incorporated into this unit, with an emphasis on: • Seeing things in the mind's eye • Self-management • Participating as a member of a team • Interpreting and communicating information	Most EFFs are incorporated into this unit, with an emphasis on: • Observing critically • Using math to solve problems and communicate • Cooperating with others • Reflecting and evaluating
• Ask and answer questions about a doctor's office • Listen and talk about a visit to the doctor • Talk about ways to get well and to stay healthy • Listen for medical advice • Listen for information to complete an appointment card • Ask and answer questions about obligations **Pronunciation:** • Listen for forms of *have* and *have to*	**L1:** 0.1.2, 3.1.1, 7.4.5, 7.4.7 **L2:** 0.1.2, 3.1.1, 3.2.3, 7.4.7 **L3:** 3.1.1, 7.1.1–7.1.3, 7.4.7 **L4:** 0.1.2, 2.3.2, 3.1.1–3.1.3, 4.8.3, 6.0.1, 7.4.7 **L5:** 3.3.1, 3.3.3, 3.4.1, 3.5.8, 3.5.9 **RE:** 0.1.2, 3.1.1, 4.8.1, 6.0.1, 7.2.5–7.2.7, 7.3.1	**L1:** 24.01–24.03, 32.01 **L2:** 24.01–24.03, 32.01, 32.02, 32.07 **L3:** 24.02, 32.01, 32.13, 33.02, 33.07 **L4:** 22.03, 24.02, 24.03, 25.01, 25.03, 32.01, 32.02, 32.13, 33.04, 33.07 **L5:** 24.02–24.04, 27.02, 32.01–32.06, 32.13 **RE:** 24.01–24.03, 32.01, 32.02, 32.05, 32.13, 33.04, 33.06, 33.07	Most SCANS are incorporated into this unit, with an emphasis on: • Seeing things in the mind's eye • Self-management • Participating as a member of a team • Acquiring and evaluating information	Most EFFs are incorporated into this unit, with an emphasis on: • Observing critically • Cooperating with others • Reflecting and evaluating • Solving problems and making decisions • Planning

Unit	Life Skills & Civics Competencies	Vocabulary	Grammar	Critical Thinking & Math Concepts	Reading & Writing
Unit 10 **Getting the Job** **page 112**	• Identify job titles • Identify job skills • Identify methods and resources for finding employment • Read help-wanted ads • Answer job interview, work history, and personal information questions • Read a time card	• Job titles • Items in a help-wanted ad • Items on a job application • Job relationships • Items on a time card	• The simple past with *be* • *Yes/No* questions with the simple past • *And/too* and *but* • *Can* and *can't*	• Interpret help-wanted ads • Analyze and describe personal work experience • Interpret a time card • Describe ability or lack of ability **Real-life math:** • Calculate pay based on time card information **Problem solving:** • Compare jobs based on salary and hours	• Read about getting a job • Write about looking for a job • Read help-wanted ads • Write answers to *Yes/No* questions using the simple past • Read a job application • Read an article about ideal employees • Read a time card • Write about work histories
Unit 11 **Safety First** **page 124**	• Identify common traffic signs • Identify workplace safety equipment • Read a safety poster • Give important information when calling 911 • Identify causes of automobile accidents • Identify safe and dangerous behavior	• Traffic signs • Workplace safety equipment • Emergencies • Road safety	• *Should* and *shouldn't* • Adverbs of frequency • Information questions with *should* • *Yes/No* questions with *should*	• Interpret traffic signs • Classify behavior as safe or unsafe • Classify language-learning habits as positive or negative • Describe emergencies to a 911 operator • Interpret a pie chart of accident data **Real-life math:** • Calculate percentages **Problem solving:** • Determine appropriate behavior following an accident	• Read traffic signs • Read about safe and dangerous behavior • Read a safety poster • Write sentences using *should* and *shouldn't* • Read an article about road safety • Write advice based on traffic signs
Unit 12 **Free Time** **page 136**	• Identify common U.S. holidays • State weather conditions • Plan leisure activities • Use public transportation schedules to make plans • Plan to see a movie • Read a phone book	• Holidays • Weather • Leisure activities • Making plans • Special occasions	• The future with *be going to* • Contractions of *be going to* • Questions, answers, and statements with *be going to*	• Classify leisure activities by season • Interpret information on a bus schedule • Interpret movie ads • Interpret information from a phone book **Real-life math:** • Calculate times in order to make plans **Problem solving:** • Determine how to modify plans due to bad weather	• Read about a trip to a baseball game • Read a bus schedule • Write questions using *be going to* • Read movie ads • Read about greeting cards • Read a page from a phone book • Write advice based on traffic signs

Listening scripts pages 148–158 **Grammar charts** pages 159–164 **Vocabulary list** pages 165–168 **Index** pages 169–172 **Map** page 173

Listening & Speaking	CASAS Life Skills Competencies	Standardized Student Syllabi/ LCPs	SCANS Competencies	EFF Content Standards
• Ask and answer questions about jobs and skills • Listen for information about a person's work history • Ask and answer questions about a help-wanted ad • Talk about pictures of people at work • Ask and answer questions about job history **Pronunciation** • *Can* and *can't*	**L1:** 0.1.2, 4.1.6, 4.1.8, 7.4.5, 7.4.7 **L2:** 0.1.2, 1.2.5, 2.5.4, 4.1.6, 4.1.8, 6.0.1, 7.4.7 **L3:** 0.1.2, 4.1.6, 4.1.8, 6.0.1, 7.4.7 **L4:** 0.1.2, 0.2.1, 4.1.6, 4.1.8, 4.4.7, 4.8.3, 6.0.1 **L5:** 2.3.2, 4.1.6, 4.1.7, 4.2.1, 4.4.1, 4.4.2, 4.4.4, 4.6.1, 6.0.1 **RE:** 0.1.2, 0.1.3, 2.5.4, 4.8.1, 6.0.1, 7.2.5–7.2.7, 7.3.1	**L1:** 18.02, 19.02, 32.01 **L2:** 19.02, 25.01, 32.01, 32.02, 32.07, 32.13, 33.02 **L3:** 18.02, 19.02, 22.01, 25.01, 32.01, 32.07, 32.13 **L4:** 18.02, 18.03, 18.06, 19.02, 22.01, 25.01, 32.01–32.03, 32.13, 33.02, 34.01–34.03 **L5:** 19.01–19.04, 20.02, 25.01, 25.03, 32.01, 32.04–32.06, 32.13 **RE:** 18.02, 19.02, 25.01, 32.01, 32.02, 32.05, 32.13, 33.02	Most SCANS are incorporated into this unit, with an emphasis on: • Seeing things in the mind's eye • Self-management • Participating as a member of a team • Acquiring and evaluating information • Interpreting and communicating information	Most EFFs are incorporated into this unit, with an emphasis on: • Observing critically • Using math to solve problems and communicate • Cooperating with others • Reflecting and evaluating
• Ask and answer questions about safety in the workplace • Listen for information about a safety checklist • Talk about safety habits at home, work, and in the car • Talk about things people should and shouldn't do • Describe emergencies • Listen for emergency information **Pronunciation:** • *Should* and *shouldn't*	**L1:** 0.1.2, 1.9.1, 2.2.2, 2.5.4, 3.4.2, 4.3.2, 4.3.3, 4.6.3, 7.4.5, 7.4.7 **L2:** 0.1.2, 0.1.3, 1.4.8, 3.4.2, 4.3.1–4.3.3, 4.6.1, 4.6.3, 6.0.1, 6.4.2, 7.4.7 **L3:** 0.1.2, 0.1.3, 3.4.2, 4.3.1, 4.3.2, 4.4.3, 4.6.1, 4.6.3, 7.4.7 **L4:** 0.1.2, 0.1.3, 1.9.7, 2.1.2, 2.5.1, 3.1.1, 4.3.4, 6.0.1, 7.4.7 **L5:** 0.1.2, 0.1.3, 1.9.7, 3.4.2, 6.0.1, 6.7.4, 7.4.5 **RE:** 0.1.2, 0.1.3, 1.4.8, 1.9.1, 1.9.7, 2.2.2, 2.4.1, 2.5.1, 3.4.2, 4.8.1, 6.0.1, 7.2.5–7.2.7, 7.3.1	**L1:** 19.01, 26.04, 27.02, 32.01 **L2:** 19.01, 25.01, 26.06, 32.01, 32.02, 32.05, 32.13, 33.08 **L3:** 32.01, 33.02, 33.07 **L4:** 23.01, 25.01, 27.01, 32.01, 32.02, 32.13 **L5:** 25.01, 26.06, 32.01, 32.03, 32.04, 32.06 **RE:** 19.01, 23.01, 26.04, 26.06, 27.01, 27.02, 32.01, 32.02, 32.05, 32.07, 33.02, 33.07	Most SCANS are incorporated into this unit, with an emphasis on: • Seeing things in the mind's eye • Self-management • Participating as a member of a team • Acquiring and evaluating information • Interpreting and communicating information	Most EFFs are incorporated into this unit, with an emphasis on: • Observing critically • Reflecting and evaluating • Solving problems and making decisions • Cooperating with others
• Ask and answer questions about leisure activities • Listen and talk about plans • Listen for information about a bus schedule • Talk about a bus schedule • Listen for information about a movie • Talk about where to find local information **Pronunciation:** • Formal and relaxed pronunciation	**L1:** 0.1.2, 0.2.4, 2.3.3, 7.4.5, 7.4.7 **L2:** 0.1.2, 0.1.3, 0.2.4, 2.2.2–2.2.4, 2.6.1, 6.0.1, 7.4.7 **L3:** 0.1.2, 0.2.4, 2.3.3, 7.4.7 **L4:** 0.1.2, 0.1.6, 0.2.4, 2.6.1–2.6.3, 6.0.1, 7.4.7 **L5:** 0.1.2, 1.1.3, 2.3.2, 2.5.3, 2.7.1, 6.0.1 **RE:** 0.1.2, 0.1.3, 2.3.3, 2.6.3, 4.8.1, 7.2.5–7.2.7, 7.3.1	**L1:** 29.04, 30.01, 32.01, 32.02, 32.13 **L2:** 22.03, 25.01, 32.01, 32.02, 32.13 **L3:** 30.01, 32.01, 33.02, 33.06, 33.09 **L4:** 25.01, 32.01, 32.02, 32.13 **L5:** 25.01, 29.04, 32.01–32.06 **RE:** 30.01, 32.01, 32.02, 32.05, 32.13, 33.02	Most SCANS are incorporated into this unit, with an emphasis on: • Seeing things in the mind's eye • Self-management • Time • Participating as a member of a team • Interpreting and communicating information	Most EFFs are incorporated into this unit, with an emphasis on: • Observing critically • Cooperating with others • Using math to solve problems and communicate

INTRODUCTION TO *STEP FORWARD*

A Word or Two About Reading Introductions to Textbooks

Teaching professionals rarely read a book's introduction. Instead, we flip through the book's pages, using the pictures, topics, and exercises to determine whether the book matches our learners' needs and our teaching style. We scan the reading passages, conversations, writing tasks, and grammar charts to judge the authenticity and accuracy of the text. At a glance, we assess how easy it would be to manage the pair work, group activities, evaluations, and application tasks.

This Introduction, however, also offers valuable information for the teacher. Because you've read this far, I encourage you to read a little further to learn how *Step Forward's* key concepts, components, and multilevel applications will help you help your learners.

Step Forward's Key Concepts

Step Forward is...

- the instructional backbone for single-level and multilevel classrooms.
- a standards-based, performance-based, and topic-based series for low-beginning through high-intermediate learners.
- a source for ready-made, four-skill lesson plans that address the skills our learners need in their workplace, civic, personal, and academic lives.
- a collection of learner-centered, communicative English-language practice activities.

The classroom is a remarkable place. *Step Forward* respects the depth of experience and knowledge that learners bring to the learning process. At the same time, *Step Forward* recognizes that learners' varied proficiencies, goals, interests, and educational backgrounds create instructional challenges for teachers.

To ensure that our learners leave each class having made progress toward their language and life goals, *Step Forward* works from these key concepts:

- **The wide spectrum of learners' needs makes using materials that support multilevel instruction essential.** *Step Forward* works with single-level and multilevel classes.
- **Learners' prior knowledge is a valuable teaching tool.** Prior knowledge questions appear in every *Step Forward* lesson.

- **Learning objectives are the cornerstone of instruction.** Each *Step Forward* lesson focuses on an objective that derives from identified learner needs, correlates to state and federal standards, and connects to a meaningful communication task. Progress toward the objective is evaluated at the end of the lesson.
- **Vocabulary, grammar, and pronunciation skills play an essential role in language learning. They provide learners with the tools needed to achieve life skill, civics, workplace, and academic competencies.** *Step Forward* includes strong vocabulary and grammar strands and features pronunciation and math lesson extensions in each unit.
- **Effective instruction requires a variety of instructional techniques and strategies to engage learners.** Techniques such as Early Production Questioning, Focused Listening, Total Physical Response (TPR), Cooperative Learning, and Problem Solving are embedded in the *Step Forward* series, along with grouping and classroom management strategies.

The *Step Forward* Program

The *Step Forward* program has five levels:

- Intro: pre-beginning
- Book 1: low-beginning
- Book 2: high-beginning
- Book 3: low-intermediate
- Book 4: intermediate to high-intermediate

Each level of *Step Forward* correlates to *The Oxford Picture Dictionary*. For pre-literacy learners, *The Basic Oxford Picture Dictionary Literacy Program* provides a flexible, needs-based approach to literacy instruction. Once learners develop strong literacy skills, they will be able to transition seamlessly into *Step Forward Introductory Level*.

Each *Step Forward* level includes the following components:

Step Forward Student Book

A collection of clear, engaging, four-skill lessons based on meaningful learning objectives.

Step Forward Audio Program

The recorded vocabulary, focused listening, conversations, pronunciation, and reading materials from the *Step Forward Student Book*.

Step Forward Step-By-Step Lesson Plans with Multilevel Grammar Exercises CD-ROM

An instructional planning resource with interleaved *Step Forward Student Book* pages, detailed lesson plans featuring multilevel teaching strategies and teaching tips, and a CD-ROM of printable multilevel grammar practice for the structures presented in the *Step Forward Student Book*.

Step Forward Workbook

Practice exercises for independent work in the classroom or as homework.

Step Forward Multilevel Activity Book

More than 100 photocopiable communicative practice activities and 72 picture cards; lesson materials that work equally well in single-level or multilevel settings.

Step Forward Test Generator CD-ROM with ExamView® Assessment Suite

Hundreds of multiple choice and life-skill oriented test items for each *Step Forward Student Book*.

Multilevel Applications of *Step Forward*

All the *Step Forward* program components support multilevel instruction.

Step Forward is so named because it helps learners "step forward" toward their language and life goals, no matter where they start. Our learners often start from very different places and language abilities within the same class.

Regardless of level, all learners need materials that bolster comprehension while providing an appropriate amount of challenge. This makes multilevel materials an instructional necessity in most classrooms.

Each *Step Forward* lesson provides the following multilevel elements:

• **a general topic or competency area** that works across levels. This supports the concept that members of the class community need to feel connected, despite their differing abilities.
• **clear, colorful visuals and realia** that provide pre-level and on-level support during introduction, presentation and practice exercises, as well as prompts for higher-level questions and exercises.

In addition, *Step Forward* correlates to *The Oxford Picture Dictionary* so that teachers can use the visuals and vocabulary from *The Oxford Picture Dictionary* to support and expand upon each lesson.

• **learner-centered practice exercises** that can be used with same-level or mixed-level pairs or small groups. *Step Forward* exercises are broken down to their simplest steps. Once the exercise has been modeled, learners can usually conduct the exercises themselves.
• **pre-level, on-level, and higher-level objectives for each lesson and the multilevel strategies** necessary to carry out the lesson. These objectives are featured in the *Step-By-Step Lesson Plans*.
• **Grammar Boost pages in the Step Forward Workbook that provide excellent "wait time" activities** for learners who complete an exercise early, thus solving a real issue in the multilevel class.
• **a variety of pair, whole class, and small group activities** in the *Step Forward Multilevel Activity Book*. These activities are perfect for same-level and mixed-level grouping.
• **customizable grammar and evaluation exercises** in the *Step Forward Test Generator CD-ROM with ExamView® Assessment Suite*. These exercises make it possible to create evaluations specific to each level in the class.

Professional Development

As instructors, we need to reflect on second language acquisition in order to build a repertoire of effective instructional strategies. The *Step Forward Professional Development Program* provides research-based teaching strategies, tasks, and activities for single- and multilevel classes.

About Writing an ESL Series

It's collaborative! *Step Forward* is the product of dialogs with hundreds of teachers and learners. The dynamic quality of language instruction makes it important to keep this dialog alive. As you use this book in your classes, I invite you to contact me or any member of the *Step Forward* authorial team with your questions or comments.

Jayme Adelson-Goldstein

Jayme Adelson-Goldstein, Series Director
Stepforwardteam.us@oup.com

**Step Forward: All you need to ensure your learners' success.
All the *Step Forward Student Books* follow this format.**

LESSON 1: VOCABULARY teaches key words and phrases relevant to the unit topic, and provides conversation practice using the target vocabulary.

New vocabulary is introduced through vibrant art and high-interest listening texts.

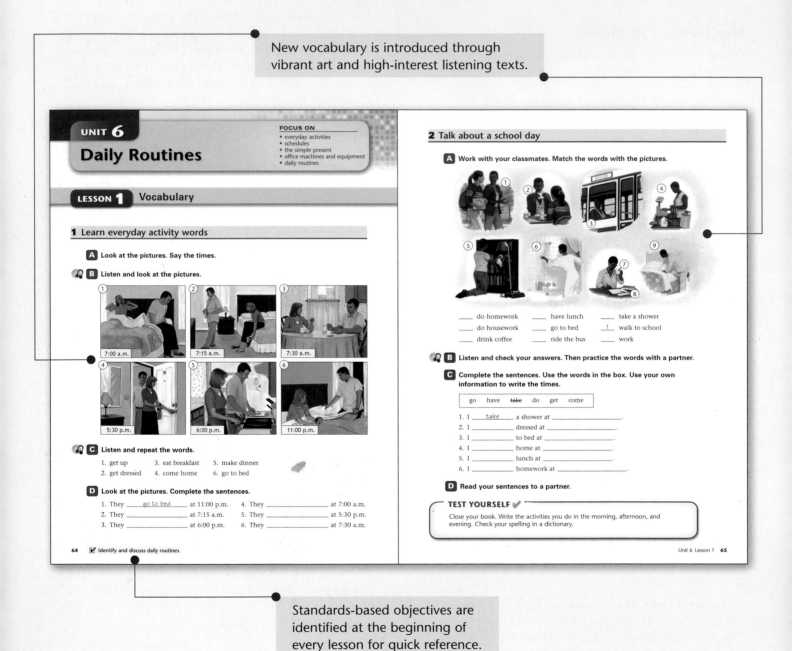

Standards-based objectives are identified at the beginning of every lesson for quick reference.

LESSON 2: LIFE STORIES expands on vocabulary learned in Lesson 1 and furthers learners' understanding through reading and writing about a life skills topic.

Life skills readings help learners practice the vocabulary in natural contexts.

Learners apply the vocabulary to their own lives by writing about their personal experiences.

LESSON 2 Life stories

1 Read about a work schedule

A Look at the pictures. Listen.

Good morning. Doctor's office.

B Listen again. Read the sentences.

1. My name is Tina Aziz. I work in a doctor's office.
2. This is my work schedule. I work from 9 a.m. to 5 p.m., Monday to Thursday.
3. I turn on the computer and copy machine at 9:00. I answer the phone all day.
4. At noon, I meet my friend. We have lunch and talk.
5. On Fridays, I don't work. I relax. I take my kids to the park.
6. I like my job and my schedule a lot, but Fridays are my favorite day.

C Check your understanding. Circle *a* or *b*.

1. Tina works ____.
   a. four days a week
   b. on Saturday

2. She answers the phone ____.
   a. at 9 a.m.
   b. all day

3. Tina and her friend have lunch ____.
   a. at 11 a.m.
   b. at 12 p.m.

4. She likes her job ____.
   a. a lot
   b. a little

---

2 Write about your schedule

A Write about your schedule. Complete the sentences.

I go to school from _____ to _____.
I study _____ at school.
On _____, I relax.
I _____.

Need help?

Ways to relax
go to the park
watch TV
listen to music
talk to friends and family
take a walk

B Read your story to a partner.

3 Talk about a work schedule

A Listen and check (✔) the activities you hear.

____ 1. mop the floor
____ 2. vacuum the rug
____ 3. answer the phone
____ 4. wash the windows
____ 5. turn on the copy machine
____ 6. help the manager

Mel at work

B Listen again. Complete Mel's work schedule.

MORNING 10 A.M.–12 P.M.	AFTERNOON 12 P.M.–3 P.M.
1. _mop the floor_	3.
2.	4.

C Listen and repeat.

A: I work on Saturday and Sunday. How about you?
B: I don't work.
A: I go to school from Monday to Friday. How about you?
B: I go to school on Monday and Wednesday.

D Work with a partner. Practice the conversation. Use your own information.

TEST YOURSELF ✔

Close your book. Listen to your partner's schedule for the week. Write the schedule you hear.

Test Yourself, at the end of every lesson, provides learners with ongoing self-assessment.

LESSON 3: GRAMMAR provides clear, simple presentation of the target structure followed by thorough, meaningful practice of it.

Clear grammar charts and exercises help learners develop language confidence and accuracy.

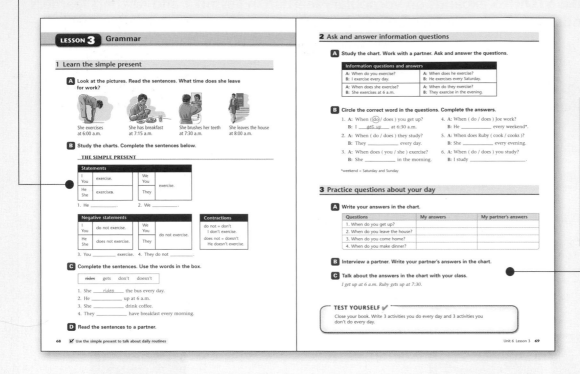

Learners work together to increase fluency and accuracy, using the grammar point to talk about themselves.

LESSON 4: EVERYDAY CONVERSATION provides learners with fluent, authentic conversations to increase familiarity with natural English.

Pronunciation activities focus on common areas of difficulty.

Listening activities build listening skills.

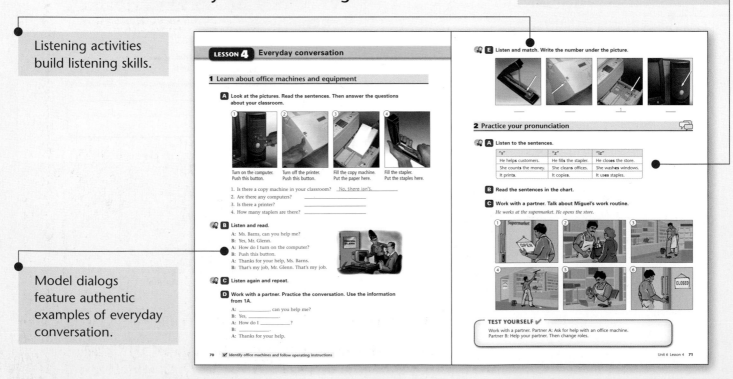

Model dialogs feature authentic examples of everyday conversation.

LESSON 5: REAL-LIFE READING develops essential reading skills and offers both life skill and pre-academic reading materials.

High-interest readings recycle vocabulary and grammar.

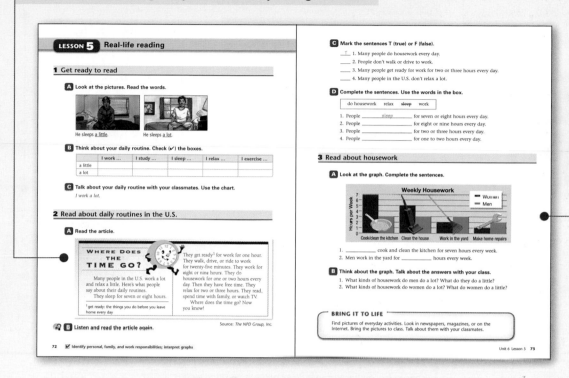

Chart literacy is increased through practice reading and understanding different types of charts.

REVIEW AND EXPAND includes additional grammar practice and communicative group tasks to ensure your learners' progress.

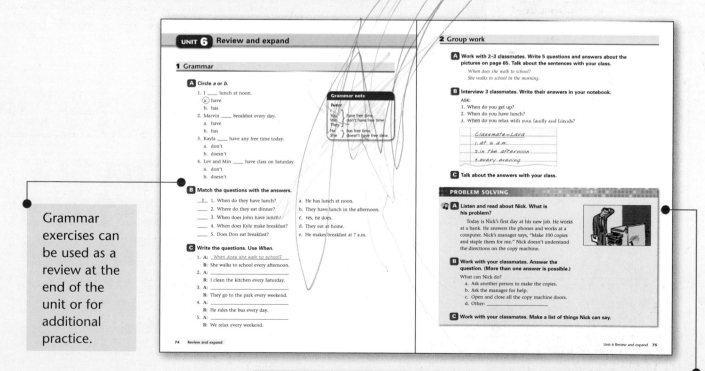

Grammar exercises can be used as a review at the end of the unit or for additional practice.

Problem solving tasks encourage learners to use critical thinking skills and meaningful discussion to find solutions to common problems.

Step Forward offers many different components.

Step-By-Step Lesson Plans

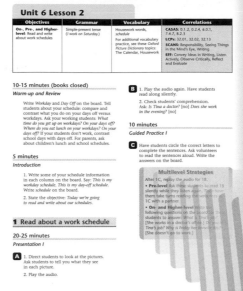

The *Step-By-Step Lesson Plans* provide tips and strategies for conducting *Student Book* activities and applying the lesson to the multilevel classroom.

Multilevel Strategies

After 1C, replay the audio for 1B.

- **Pre-level** Ask these students to read 1B silently while they listen again. Then have them take turns reading the sentences in 1C with a partner.

- **On- and Higher-level** Write the following questions on the board for these students to answer: What is Tina's job? [She works in a doctor's office.] Do you like Tina's job? Why is Friday her favorite day? [She doesn't go to work.]

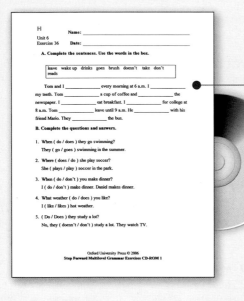

The *Multilevel Grammar Exercises CD-ROM*, a free CD-ROM included with the *Step-By-Step Lesson Plans*, offers additional exercises for pre-level, on-level, and higher-level learners for each grammar point in the *Student Book*.

Workbook

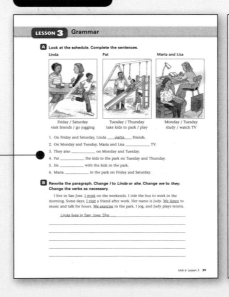

The *Workbook* offers additional exercises ideal for independent practice, homework, or review.

Multilevel Activity Book

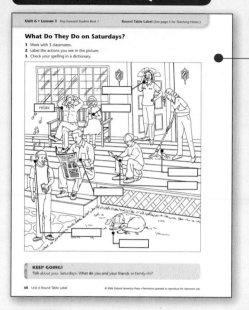

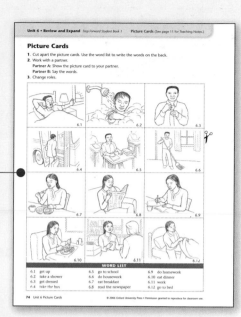

The *Multilevel Activity Book* features over 100 reproducible communication activities to complement the multilevel classroom through a variety of pair, small group, and whole-class activities.

There are over 140 picture cards in the *Multilevel Activity Book* that are perfect for practicing key vocabulary and grammar.

Audio Program

Audio CDs and Cassettes feature the listening exercises from the *Student Book* as well as conversations, pronunciation, and readings.

Test Generator

The *Test Generator CD-ROM with ExamView® Assessment Suite* offers hundreds of test items for each *Student Book*. Teachers can print out ready-made tests or create their own tests.

Professional Development

Professional Development Task 8

Imagine you want your learners to practice listening carefully during a group task. One behavior you could demonstrate would be leaning forward. Make a list of at least three other behaviors or expressions that careful listeners use.

The *Professional Development Program* offers instructors research-based teaching strategies and activities for single- and multilevel classes, plus Professional Development Tasks like this one.

The First Step

Names and Numbers

1 Spell your name

  A **Listen and look at the pictures.**

1. Point to a letter.
2. Say your name. — Tom.
3. Spell your name. — T-O-M.

  B **Listen and repeat.**

The Alphabet								
A	B	C	D	E	F	G	H	I
a	b	c	d	e	f	g	h	i
J	K	L	M	N	O	P	Q	R
j	k	l	m	n	o	p	q	r
S	T	U	V	W	X	Y	Z	
s	t	u	v	w	x	y	z	

  C **Listen and spell the names.**

1. M a r i a
2. L e __
3. T __ __
4. R __ b __ __ __ a
5. K __ m a __
6. __ a __ i __

D **Work with 2–3 classmates. Say and spell your name.**

A: *I'm Jack.*
B: *Please spell that.*
A: *J-A-C-K.*

A: *I'm Carmen.*
B: *Excuse me. I don't understand.*
A: *I'm Carmen. C-A-R-M-E-N.*

2 Learn numbers

A Listen and say the numbers.

1	2	3	4	5
one	two	three	four	five

6	7	8	9	10
six	seven	eight	nine	ten

11	12	13	14	15
eleven	twelve	thirteen	fourteen	fifteen

16	17	18	19	20
sixteen	seventeen	eighteen	nineteen	twenty

> **Need help?**
>
> **0 = zero**
> You can say "O" instead of "zero" in phone numbers and addresses.

B Work with a partner. Partner A: Say a phone number. Partner B: Listen and write the phone number.

1. 555-3611
2. 555-1468
3. (213) 555-8837
4. (714) 555-9592

5-5-5-4-3-2-1

phone number

C Work with a partner. Partner A: Say an address. Partner B: Listen and write the address.

1. 1711 G Street
2. 1214 B Street
3. 613 K Street
4. 1516 Q Street

address

3 Learn more numbers

A Listen and count from 20 to 30.

20　21　22　23　24　25　26　27　28　29　30

B Listen and count by tens.

10	20	30	40	50
ten	twenty	thirty	forty	fifty

60	70	80	90	100
sixty	seventy	eighty	ninety	one hundred

C Listen and write the numbers.

1. _____
2. _____
3. _____
4. _____

UNIT 1

In the Classroom

FOCUS ON
- classroom English
- personal information
- the verb *be*
- meeting people
- study goals

LESSON 1 — Vocabulary

1 Learn classroom directions

A Look at the pictures. Say the letters.

B Listen and look at the pictures.

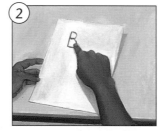

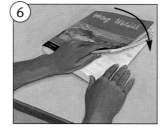

C Listen and repeat the words.

1. listen to
2. point to
3. say
4. repeat
5. open
6. close
7. sit down
8. stand up

D Look at the pictures. Complete the sentences.
Use the words in the box.

Point	Sit	Say	Close	Listen to	Stand	~~Open~~	Repeat

1. _Open_ the notebook.
2. _repeat_ the letter D.
3. _open_ the book, please.
4. _point_ to the letter B.
5. _Sit_ down, please.
6. _Stand_ up, please.
7. _Say_ the letter C.
8. _listen to_ the letter A.

2 Talk about a classroom

A Work with your classmates. Match the words with the picture.

_1_ board	_10_ chairs	_8_ desk	_6_ notebooks	_4_ students
_8_ books	_3_ clock	_5_ dictionary	_7_ pens	_2_ teacher

B Listen and check your answers. Then practice the words with a partner.

C Complete the chart.

Singular	Plural
a desk	desks
a chair	books
a teacher	chairs
Clock	boards
board	notebooks

Grammar note

Singular (1)	Plural (2, 3, 4 . . .)
a pen	pens
a book	books
a student	students

D Work with a partner. Give classroom directions.

A: *Say "book."*

B: *Book.*

TEST YOURSELF ✔

Close your book. Write 3 classroom directions. Write 3 words for things or people in the classroom. Check your spelling in a dictionary.

1 Read about school forms

A **Look at the pictures. Listen.**

School Registration Form

Name:
1. <u>Jim</u>   <u>Santos</u>
   (first)   (last)

Address:
2. <u>27 Lima Street, Apartment 3</u>
   (street)

   <u>Dallas,</u>   <u>Texas</u>   <u>75202</u>
   (city)   (state)   (zip code)

Telephone:
3. <u>(214) 555-1204</u>
   (area code)

Email:
4. <u>jsantos@work.net</u>

Signature:
5. <u>Jim Santos</u>

B **Listen. Read the sentences.**

1. Tell me your first name. Please spell your last name.
2. Complete the form. Please print your address.
3. Write your telephone number with the area code.
   Then write your email address.
4. Sign your name on line five.
5. Please give me the form. Welcome to school.

C **Check your understanding. Match the numbers with the letters.**

<u>b</u> 1. tell   a. (J-I-M.)

____ 2. spell   b. (Jim.)

____ 3. print   c. *Jim Santos*

____ 4. sign   d. Jim Santos

2 Complete a form

A Write your information on the form. Sign your name on line 3.

1. Name: _____
             (FIRST)   (LAST)

2. Telephone: (_____) _____
           (AREA CODE)

3. Signature: _____

B Read your information to a partner.

3 Give personal information

A Listen and circle *a* or *b*.

Jose Ramirez
16 Elm Street
Los Angeles, CA 90011
(323) 555-1242

1. a. Elm Street
   (b.) Ramirez

2. a. 555-1242
   b. 16

3. a. (323)
   b. 90011

4. a. 16 Elm Street
   b. joseram@123.net

5. a. Jose
   b. Ramirez

6. a. Los Angeles
   b. *Jose Ramirez*

B Listen and write.

1. _____
2. _____
3. _____
4. _____
5. _____
6. _____

C Listen and repeat.

A: Tell me your first name.
B: Maria.

A: Please spell your last name.
B: G-O-N-Z-A-L-E-S.

D Work with a partner. Practice the conversation.
Use your own information.

TEST YOURSELF ✔

Close your book. Write your address and your phone number.

1 Learn the verb *be*

A Look at the pictures. Read the sentences. Count the students in each picture.

My Class

I am a student.　　He is my teacher.　　She is my partner.　　They are　　　　　We are a group.　　It is my classroom.
　　　　　　　　　　　　　　　　　　　　　　　　　　　　　my classmates.

B Study the charts. Complete the sentences below.

STATEMENTS WITH *BE*

Statements						
I	am	a student.	We		are	students.
You	are		You			
He She	is		They			
It	is	my classroom.	They		are	my books.

1. I _____ a student.　　2. They _____ students.

Negative statements						
I	am not	a student.	We		are not	students.
You	are not		You			
He She	is not		They			
It	is not	my classroom.	They		are not	my books.

3. He _____ a student.　　4. They _____ my books.

C Work with your classmates. Talk about your classroom.

I am a student.　　　　　*They are my books.*
She is not a teacher.　　*It is not my pen.*

☑ Use subject pronouns and the simple present with *be* to talk about the classroom

2 Contractions with *be*

A Study the chart. Circle the correct words below.

Contractions				
I am	=	I'm		
you are	=	you're		
he is	=	he's		
she is	=	she's		
it is	=	it's		
we are	=	we're		
they are	=	they're		

I am not	=	I'm not
you are not	=	you're not / you aren't
he is not	=	he's not / he isn't
she is not	=	she's not / she isn't
it is not	=	it's not / it isn't
we are not	=	we're not / we aren't
they are not	=	they're not / they aren't

1. (**I'm** / They're) a student.
2. (She's / It's) a teacher.
3. (He's / It's) a pen.
4. (He's / I'm) my partner.
5. (It isn't / They aren't) my books.
6. He (isn't / aren't) a teacher.

B Work with a partner. Talk about your classroom. Use contractions.

A: *He's a student.*
B: *They're books.*

3 Practice statements with *be*

A Read the words.

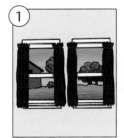     

1. windows   2. a computer   3. pencils   4. a door   5. a new student   6. a teacher

B Work with a partner. Talk about the pictures.

A: *They're windows.*
B: *It's a computer.*

TEST YOURSELF ✔

Close your book. Write 5 sentences about your classroom. Read your sentences to a partner.

LESSON 4 Everyday conversation

1 Learn how to meet new people

 A Listen and read the conversations.

B Complete the conversations.

1. **A:** Hi, I'm Li. What is your name?
   B: My ___name___ is Neela.

2. **A:** It's nice to meet _____, Neela.
   B: It's nice to meet you, _____.

3. **A:** _____, Neela.
   B: Good morning, Li.

4. **A:** _____ are _____?
   B: _____, thanks. And you?
   A: Fine.

5. **A:** _____ evening, Neela.
   B: Hello, Li.

6. **A:** See you _____, Neela.
   B: _____, Li.

 C Listen and read.

A: Hi, I'm Tim. What is your name?
B: My name is Asha. This is my friend Sara.
A: Can you repeat that, please?
B: Yes. I'm Asha, and this is Sara. It's nice to meet you.
A: Nice to meet you, too. Who is your teacher?
B: Ms. Simpson.
A: Oh! She's my teacher, too.

 D Listen again and repeat.

10   ✔ Begin and end social conversations

E **Work with a partner. Practice the conversation.**
Use your own information.

A: Hi, I'm _____. What is your name?

B: My name is _____.

A: Can you repeat that, please?

B: I'm _____. It's nice to meet you, _____.

A: Nice to meet you, too. Who is your teacher?

B: _____.

A: Oh! _____ my teacher, too.

2 Practice your pronunciation

  A **Study the chart. Listen for the contractions.**

No contraction	Contraction
What is your name?	What**'s** your name?
I am Maria.	I**'m** Maria.
Who is your teacher?	Who**'s** your teacher?

  B **Listen and check (✔) *no contraction* or *contraction*.**

	No contraction	Contraction
1.	✔	
2.		
3.		
4.		
5.		

C **Work with your classmates. Ask and answer the questions.**

1. A: What's your name?

   B: My name is _____.

2. A: How are you?

   B: I'm _____.

3. A: Who's your teacher?

   B: My teacher is _____.

┌─ **TEST YOURSELF** ✔ ─────────────────

Work with a partner. Partner A: Say hello to your partner and say your
name. Ask your partner's name. Partner B: Answer the question and say
goodbye. Then change roles.

1 Get ready to read

A Look at the pictures. Read the sentences.

☐ Read English.

☐ Go to school.

I'm a student.

☐ Speak English.

☐ Ask for help.

B How do you study English? Check (✔) the boxes in 1A.

2 Read about studying English

A Read the poster.

Learn more English.

Study every day.

Good morning.

Speak English at home.

Go to school.

Today in the news…

Listen to English on the radio.

Ask your classmates and teacher for help.

B Listen and read the poster again.

✔ Identify effective language-learning habits

C Circle *a* or *b*.

1. Ask your ____ for help.
    a. teacher
    b. pencil

2. ____ to English on the radio.
    a. Speak
    b. Listen

D Complete the sentences. Use the words in the box.

| English   school   help   ~~study~~ |

1. _Study_____ every day.
2. Learn more _____.
3. Go to _____.
4. Ask your classmates for _____.

3 Name your goals

A Complete the form.

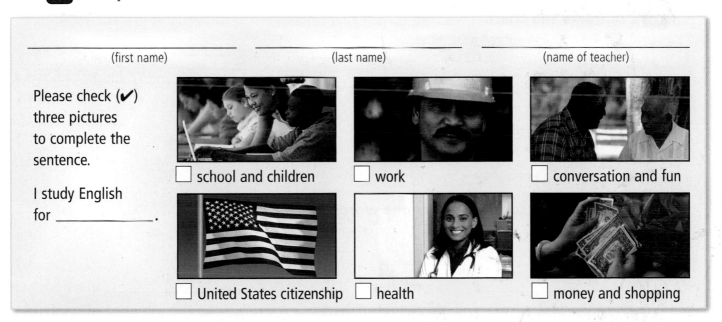

| (first name) | (last name) | (name of teacher) |

Please check (✔) three pictures to complete the sentence.

I study English for _____.

☐ school and children   ☐ work   ☐ conversation and fun

☐ United States citizenship   ☐ health   ☐ money and shopping

B Work with your classmates. Count the checks (✔) for each picture.

┌─ **BRING IT TO LIFE** ───────────────
│ Speak English at home or with your friends for 5 minutes today.
└──────────────────────────────────

1 Grammar

A Circle *a* or *b*.

1. What are they?
   a. It's a pen.
   b. They're notebooks.

2. Who is he?
   a. It's a window.
   b. He's my teacher.

3. What are they?
   a. They're desks.
   b. She's a student.

4. Who is your friend?
   a. He's Mark.
   b. It's my pen.

> **Grammar note**
>
> **For people: *Who***
>
> A: Who is she?   A: Who are they?
> B: She's my teacher. B: They're my friends.
>
> **For things: *What***
>
> A: What is it?   A: What are they?
> B: It's my book.   B: They're my books.

B Complete the chart.

Singular	Plural
a book	books
	pencils
a desk	
	windows
a teacher	

C Complete the sentences. Use the words in the box.

| I   My books   ~~Maria~~   We |

1. ___Maria_____ is a teacher.
2. _____ am a good student.
3. _____ are students.
4. _____ are open.

D Write new sentences. Use contractions.

1. We are students. _We're students._____
2. She is at work. _____
3. They are not new computers. _____
4. It is a window. _____

2 Group work

A Work with 2–3 classmates. Look at the picture on page 5.
Write 5 sentences about the picture in your notebook.
Talk about the sentences with your class.

They are pens.
It's a desk.

B Interview a partner. Write your partner's answers in your notebook.

ASK OR SAY:

1. What is your first name?
2. What is your last name?
3. Please sign your name here.

1. Dora
2. Sanchez
3. Dora Sanchez

PROBLEM SOLVING

A Listen and read. Look at the picture.
What is the problem?

Today is the first day of class at Pass Street
Adult School. The teacher is Nora Jackson.
Jose Ortiz is a student.

B Work with your classmates. Answer the
question.

What can Jose say to Nora Jackson?
   a. Good morning.
   b. Good evening. I'm Jose Ortiz.
   c. See you later, Nora.

UNIT 2

My Classmates

FOCUS ON
- time and dates
- personal information
- *yes/no* questions with *be*
- completing a form
- countries and population

LESSON 1 Vocabulary

1 Learn the time

A Look at the pictures. Count the clocks.

STUDENT AUDIO **B** Listen and look at the pictures.

1. Good morning.
8:00 a.m.

2. 9:15 a.m.

3. 12:00 p.m.

4. Good evening.
8:30 p.m.

5. 9:45 p.m.

6. Good night.
12:00 a.m.

STUDENT AUDIO **C** Listen and repeat the words.

1. eight o'clock
2. nine fifteen a.m.
3. noon
4. eight thirty p.m.
5. nine forty-five p.m.
6. midnight

D Match the sentences with the times.

___e___ 1. It's eight o'clock in the morning.
_____ 2. It's midnight.
_____ 3. It's eight thirty in the evening.
_____ 4. It's nine forty-five in the evening.
_____ 5. It's noon.

a. 8:30 p.m.
b. 9:45 p.m.
c. 12:00 a.m.
d. 12:00 p.m.
e. 8:00 a.m.

Need help?

8:00 a.m. *or*
   8:00 in the morning

12:00 p.m. *or* noon

8:30 p.m. *or*
   8:30 in the evening

12:00 a.m. *or* midnight

2 Talk about a calendar

A Work with your classmates. Match the words with the pictures.

Start English Class 3/8/07 — ③

①—**MARCH**

②

Sunday	Monday	Tuesday	Wednesday	Thursday	Friday	Saturday
		④		1	2	3
4	5 ⑤	⑥ 6	7 ⑦	8	9	10

⑧

January	February	March	April	May	June
July	August	September	October	November	December

___ date   _1_ month   ___ tomorrow   ___ year

___ day   ___ today   ___ week   ___ yesterday

B Listen and check your answers. Then practice the words with a partner.

C Complete the chart. Use the words in the box.

Years	~~Times~~	Days	Months

Times			
5:00	Monday	January	1870
7:30	Wednesday	March	1999
12:10	Friday	September	2015

D Work with a partner. Ask and answer the questions.

1. What time is it?
2. What are the days of the week?
3. What day is today?
4. What day is tomorrow?
5. What are the months of the year?

TEST YOURSELF ✔

Close your book. Write 4 time words and 4 calendar words. Check your spelling in a dictionary.

1 Read about a student

  A **Look at the pictures. Listen.**

 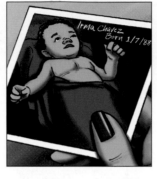  

My favorite color is purple.

B **Listen again. Read the sentences.**

1. My name is Irma Chavez.
2. I live in California.
3. I'm from Mexico.
4. My date of birth is January 7th, 1988.
5. My favorite color is purple.
6. I'm a student at City Community College.

C **Check your understanding. Circle the correct words.**

1. Irma is a (student / teacher).
2. She is from (California / Mexico).
3. She lives in (California / Mexico).
4. Irma's favorite color is (purple / green).

2 Write about your life

A **Write your story. Complete the sentences.**

My name is _____.

I live in _____.

I am from _____.

My date of birth is _____.

My favorite color is _____.

B **Read your story to a partner.**

Need help?

Colors

■ red	■ orange	☐ tan
■ blue	■ purple	■ gray
☐ yellow	■ pink	☐ white
■ green	■ brown	■ black

A Listen and number the ID cards.

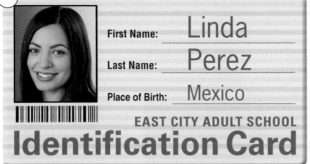

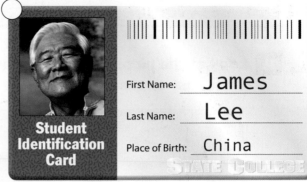

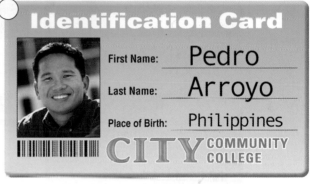

  B Listen and complete the questions.

1. What's your _____ name _____?
2. _____ are you from?
3. What's your _____ of birth?
4. What's your favorite _____?

Grammar note

Information questions with *be*

What's { your name?
your address?
your favorite color? }

Where are you from?

  C Listen and repeat.

A: What's your name?

B: My name is Tara. What's your name?

A: My name is Jun Sook. Where are you from?

B: I'm from India. Where are you from?

A: I'm from Korea.

D Work with a partner. Practice the conversation. Use your own information.

TEST YOURSELF ✓

Ask 3 classmates:

What's your name?   What's your date of birth?   What's your place of birth?

1 Learn *Yes/No* questions and answers

A Look at the pictures. Read the questions and answers.
Then answer the question: How do *you* feel?

A: Is Trang happy?
B: Yes, he is.

A: Is Maria worried?
B: Yes, she is.

A: Is the dog hungry?
B: Yes, it is.

A: Are Raj and Padma worried?
B: No, they aren't. They're proud.

A: Is Jake happy?
B: No, he isn't. He's angry.

A: Is Paul angry?
B: No, he isn't. He's tired.

B Study the charts. Complete the questions and answers below.

YES/NO QUESTIONS WITH BE

Questions		
Are	you	
Is	he she it	hungry?
Are	you they	

Answers				
Yes,	I am.	No,	I'm not.
	he is. she is. it is.		he isn't. she isn't. it isn't.
	we are. they are.		we aren't. they aren't.

1. **A:** _____ she hungry?

   B: _____, she is.

2. **A:** _____ they hungry?

   B: No, they _____.

C Look at the pictures in 1A. Ask and answer the questions.

A: *Is Trang happy?*
B: *Yes, he is.*

✔ Ask and answer *Yes/No* questions with *be*

2 Ask and answer *Yes/No questions*

A Match the questions with the answers.

<u>b</u> 1. Is Jake happy?

_____ 2. Is Maria happy?

_____ 3. Are you a student?

_____ 4. Are Raj and Padma angry?

_____ 5. Is the dog hungry?

a. Yes, I am.

b. No, he isn't. He's angry.

c. Yes, it is.

d. No, she isn't. She's worried.

e. No, they aren't. They're proud.

B Look at the chart. Answer the questions about Trang, Maria, and Paul.

Questions	Trang	Maria	Paul
Are you a teacher?	No	Yes	Yes
Are you from Mexico?	No	Yes	No
Are you hungry?	Yes	No	Yes

1. Is Paul a teacher? <u>Yes, he is.</u>

2. Is Maria hungry? _____

3. Are Trang and Paul from Mexico? _____

4. Is Maria a teacher? _____

5. Are Trang and Paul hungry? _____

3 Practice *Yes/No questions*

A Complete the questions with your own ideas. Write your answers.

Questions	You	Classmate 1	Classmate 2
1. Are you a ___student___?			yes
2. Are you from _____?			
3. Are you _____ today?			

B Interview 2 classmates. Write your classmates' answers in the chart.

C Talk about the answers in the chart with your class.

Rafael is a student. He's from Brazil. He's happy today.

TEST YOURSELF ✔

Close your book. Write 3 *Yes/No* questions. Ask and answer the questions with a partner.

1 Learn to talk about marital status

A Look at the pictures. Read the sentences. Then answer the questions below.

I'm single.

I'm single.

We're married.

Ms. Garcia is a single woman. She isn't married.

Mr. Moloto is a single man. He isn't married.

Mr. and Mrs. Kim are a married couple. They aren't single.

1. Are you single? _____

2. Are you married? _____

STUDENT AUDIO

B Listen and read.

A: Can you help me with this form?
B: Sure. Write your first name here.
A: OK.
B: Are you married or single?
A: I'm married.
B: OK, Mrs. Lee. Fill in the "married" bubble.
A: Thank you.

First name:
_____

Last name:
Lee

Title: ○ Mr. ○ Ms. ○ Mrs.
Marital status: ○ married
○ single
Place of birth: **China**
Phone: **(213) 555-2178**

 C Listen again and repeat.

D Work with a partner. Practice the conversation. Use your own information.

A: Can you help me with this form?
B: Sure. Write your first name here.
A: OK.
B: Are you married or single?
A: I'm _____.
B: OK, _____. Fill in the _____ bubble.

Need help?

Mrs. = a married woman
Miss = a single woman
Ms. = a married or single woman

Mr. = a married or single man

E Listen and write the correct title for each name.

1. _Mrs._ Pat Tyson
2. _____ Pat Song
3. _____ Terry Miller
4. _____ Terry Farmer
5. _____ Jean Silver
6. _____ Gene Gold

2 More questions with *be*

A Study the charts. Listen and repeat the questions.

Information questions
Where is Mrs. Lee from?
What's your name?

Yes/No questions
Is she a student?
Are you a student?

Or questions
Is she married or single?
Are you married or single?

B Listen and complete the missing information.

REGISTRATION FORM

Date: _____

First name: _____   Last name: _Milovich_____

Title: ☐ Mr. ☐ Ms. ☐ Mrs.

Marital status: ☐ married ☐ single

Date of birth: _____   Place of birth: _Russia_____

Address: _1769 Rose Ave._____   Phone: _____
_____ Chicago, IL 60601____

C Match the questions with the answers.

_c_ 1. What's your first name?   a. (213) 555-3954
___ 2. What's your last name?   b. 198 Second St.
___ 3. Are you married or single?   c. Pat
___ 4. What's your phone number?   d. married
___ 5. What's your address?   e. Singapore
___ 6. Where are you from?   f. Miller

TEST YOURSELF ✓

Work with a partner. Partner A: Ask the questions from 2C. Partner B: Answer the questions. Use the information on the form in 2B or your information. Then change roles.

1 Get ready to read

A Look at the pictures. Read the words.

countries

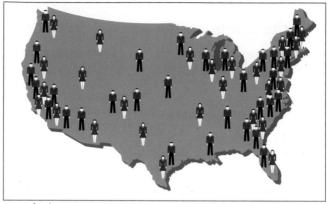

population

B Find your home country on a map. What countries are your classmates from?

2 Read about the population in the U.S.

A Read the article.

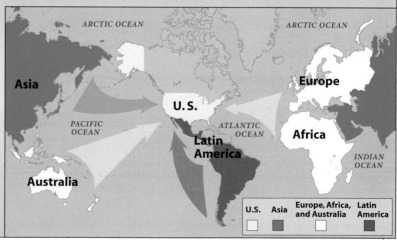

People in the United States: Where are they from?

The population of the United States is about 295 million[1] people. Today, 32.5 million people in the U.S. are from other countries. Where are they from?

- Seventeen million are from Latin America.
- Eight million are from Asia.
- Seven million are from Europe, Africa, and Australia.

---

[1] million = 1,000,000

Source: *U.S. Department of Commerce*

STUDENT AUDIO

B Listen and read the article again.

C Mark the sentences T (true) or F (false).

_____ 1. 295 million people in the U.S. are from other countries.

_____ 2. Seventeen million people in the U.S. are from Latin America.

_____ 3. Seventy-eight million people in the U.S. are from Europe.

D Complete the sentences. Use the words in the box.

| million   population   countries |

1. Many people in the U.S. are from other _____.
2. Eight _____ people in the U.S. are from Asia.
3. The U.S. _____ from Latin America is seventeen million.

3 Real-life math

A Look at the graph. What countries are people in the U.S. from?

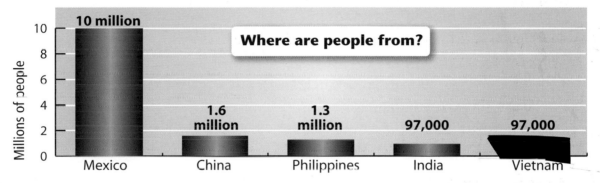

B Work with your classmates. Make a graph about your class.

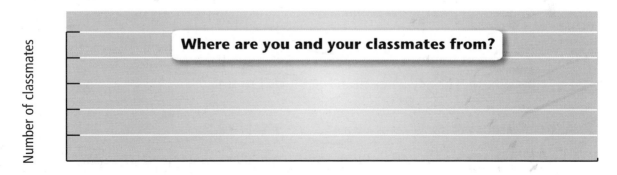

C Write sentences about your graph.

Seven students in my class are from Korea.

BRING IT TO LIFE

Ask a person NOT in your class: What's your name?   Where are you from?
Write the answers in your notebook. Talk about the answers with your classmates.

1 Grammar

A Circle *a* or *b*.

1. _____ she a student?
   a. Is *(circled)*
   b. Are

2. _____ they worried?
   a. Is
   b. Are

3. Are _____ from Japan?
   a. Li
   b. you

4. Is _____ at school today?
   a. Ms. Baker
   b. Mr. and Mrs. Jones

B Complete the questions. Use the words in the box.

What	Where	~~Who~~	Are

1. _Who_ is she?
2. _Where_ are you from?
3. _Are_ you married or single?
4. _What_ is your name?

C _____ e questions with the answers.

_d_ 1. Where are you from?   a. I'm married.

____ 2. What is your phone number? b. Yes, I am.

____ 3. Are you married or single? c. It's 555-9134.

____ 4. How are you?   d. I'm from Mexico.

____ 5. Are you hungry?   e. She's from Miami.

____ 6. Where is the teacher from? f. I'm fine.

D Write the answers.

1. Are you a student? _Yes, I am._

2. What is your first name? _____

3. What time is it? _____

4. Is today Monday? _____

5. What is your date of birth? _____

2 Group work

A Work with your classmates. Write 5 sentences about the calendar on page 17. Talk about the sentences with your class.

It's Tuesday.
The month is March.

B Interview 3 classmates. Write their answers in your notebook.

ASK:
1. Where are you from?
2. Are you married or single?
3. What's your favorite color?

Classmate—Javier
1. He's from Chile.
2. He's married.
3. It's green.

C Talk about the answers with your class.

PROBLEM SOLVING

A Look at the picture. What is the problem?

B Work with your classmates. Answer the question. (More than one answer is possible.)

What can Bella do?
    a. Give the form to the teacher.
    b. Read the form to the teacher.
    c. Ask for a new form.
    d. Other: _____

OH, NO!

Please give me your form.

Family and Friends

FOCUS ON
• family members
• descriptions of people
• possessives
• dates and phone messages
• families in the U.S.

LESSON **1** Vocabulary

1 Learn about family members

A Look at the pictures. Read and say the names and the dates.

B Listen and look at the pictures.

The Martinez Family

Carlos and Anita are married! 6/22/97

Carlos and baby Eric 11/15/99

Anita and baby Robin 4/20/03

Carlos, Anita, Eric, and Robin 6/30/06

C Listen and repeat the words.

1. wife	3. father	5. mother	7. parents
2. husband	4. son	6. daughter	8. children*

*one child / two children

D Look at the pictures. Complete the sentences.

1. Anita is a ___wife___ and ___mother___.
2. Eric is a _____.
3. Eric and Robin are _____.
4. Carlos is a _____ and _____.
5. Carlos and Anita are _____.
6. Robin is a _____.

☑ Identify family members

2 Talk about a family

A Work with your classmates. Number the people in Eric's family.

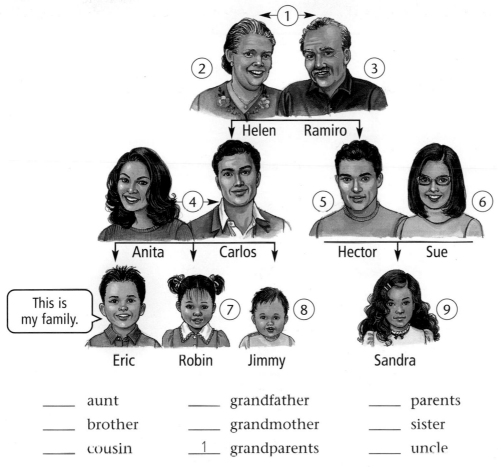

___	aunt	___	grandfather	___	parents
___	brother	___	grandmother	___	sister
___	cousin	_1_	grandparents	___	uncle

B Listen and check your answers. Then practice the words with a partner.

C Look at the picture. Complete the sentences.

1. I'm Eric's uncle. Carlos is my brother. I'm ___Hector___.

2. Eric and Jimmy are my brothers. I'm _____.

3. Anita is my aunt. Sue is my mother. I'm _____.

4. Eric is my grandson. Ramiro is my husband. I'm _____.

D Work with a partner. Tell your partner 2 things about yourself.

A: I'm a mother and an aunt. How about you?

B: I'm a grandfather and a husband.

> **Grammar note**
>
> *a or an?*
>
> a father   an aunt

TEST YOURSELF ✔

Close your book. Write 10 words for family members. Write *M* (man), *W* (woman), or *B* (both) next to each. Check your spelling in a dictionary.

1 Read about a family

  A **Look at the pictures. Listen.**

Sam

Karina

Simon

 B **Listen again. Read the sentences.**

1. My name is Paulina Gutman. These are photos of my family.
2. Sam is my son. He is the tall boy with blond hair.
3. Karina is my daughter. She is the girl with brown hair and big blue eyes.
4. My husband is the short man with beautiful gray hair. His name is Simon.
5. They are all very special to me.

C **Check your understanding. Match the numbers with the letters.**

_d_ 1. Paulina	a. brown hair and blue eyes	
____ 2. Karina	b. short with gray hair	
____ 3. Simon	c. tall with blond hair	
____ 4. Sam	d. blond hair and blue eyes	

2 Write about yourself

A Write your story. Complete the sentences.

My name is _____.

My eyes are _____.

My hair is _____.

B Read your story to a partner.

3 Describe family members

A Listen to the sentences. Then complete the chart.

Names	Family members	Hair	Eyes
1. Simon	Paulina's husband	gray	brown
2.	Paulina's		
3.	Paulina's		

B Work with a partner. Talk about the pictures in 1A. Tell your partner *Point to....*

A: Point to the thin man with gray hair.

B: Point to the attractive girl with blue eyes.

More words to describe people

attractive   young   heavy   average   thin

C Listen and repeat.

A: What color are your eyes?   A: What color is your hair?

B: My eyes are blue.   B: My hair is brown.

D Work with a partner. Practice the conversations. Use your own information.

TEST YOURSELF ✔

Close your book. Make a chart about 3 people you know. Write their names, hair color, and eye color.

1 Learn possessives

A Listen and read Joe's story. Complete the sentences below.

> My name is Joe. This is my daughter. Her name is Grace. This is my grandson. He is a great kid. His name is Charlie. Charlie's eyes are brown. His hair is blond. My eyes are green, but brown eyes are my favorite.

1. Charlie's eyes are _____.   2. His hair is _____.

B Study the chart. Then complete the sentences below. Use the words in parentheses.

POSSESSIVE ADJECTIVES

Pronouns	Possessive adjectives	Examples
I	my	My eyes are green.
you	your	Your eyes are blue.
he	his	His eyes are brown.
she	her	Her eyes are blue.
it	its	Its eyes are yellow.
we	our	Our eyes are blue.
you	your	Your eyes are brown.
they	their	Their eyes are green.

1. __My_____ eyes are green. (I)   3. _____ eyes are blue. (we)
2. _____ eyes are brown. (he)   4. _____ eyes are green. (they)

C Look at the pictures in 1A. Circle the correct words.

1. ((Her) / Their) name is Grace.
2. (His / Her) name is Charlie. His hair (is / are) blond.
3. (Their / Your) names (is / are) Grace and Charlie.
4. Grace is a mother. Charlie is (his / her) son.

☑ Use possessive nouns and adjectives to describe people

2 Ask and answer information questions with possessives

A Study the chart. Listen and repeat the questions and answers.

Information questions and answers with possessives		Notes:
A: What color is Charlie's hair? **B:** His hair is blond.	**A:** What color is Grace's hair? **B:** Her hair is blond.	Use **'s** after a name for the possessive.
A: What color are Charlie's eyes? **B:** His eyes are brown.	**A:** What color are Grace's eyes? **B:** Her eyes are blue.	Charlie**'s** eyes = his eyes Mary**'s** book = her book Mr. Smith**'s** pen = his pen

B Complete the answers.

1. **A:** Who is Charlie's grandfather?

   B: _His_ name is Joe.

2. **A:** Who is Joe's grandson?

   B: Charlie is _____ grandson.

3. **A:** What is his daughter's name?

   B: _____ name is Grace.

4. **A:** What is your teacher's name?

   B: _____ teacher's name is _____.

C Underline the possessive names. Write new sentences.

1. <u>Grace's</u> hair is blond.   _Her hair is blond._

2. Joe's eyes are green.   _____

3. Paulina's children are tall.   _____

4. Grace and Charlie's dog is brown.   _____

3 Practice possessives

A Read the questions. Write your answers in the chart.

Questions	My answers	My partner's answers
1. What's your name?		
2. What color are your eyes?		
3. What color is your hair?		

B Interview a partner. Write your partner's answers in the chart.

C Talk about the answers in the chart with your class.

His name is Asim. Asim's eyes are green. His hair is black.

TEST YOURSELF ✔

Close your book. Write 4 sentences. Describe your classmates and your teacher.
My teacher's hair is brown.

1 Learn to read and say dates

  A Listen and read the calendar. Then complete the sentences below.

March

Sun.	Mon.	Tues.	Wed.	Thurs.	Fri.	Sat.
		1st	2nd Ashley	3rd	4th	5th
6th	7th	8th	9th	10th	11th	12th
13th	14th	15th	16th	17th	18th	19th
20th The first day of spring	21st	22nd	23rd Julie	24th	25th	26th
27th	28th	29th	30th	31st		

Need help?

Months of the year

January	July
February	August
March	September
April	October
May	November
June	December

Dates

1st = first
2nd = second
3rd = third
4th = fourth
5th = fifth
20th = twentieth
21st = twenty-first

1. Ashley's birthday is on _____.

2. The first day of spring is on _____.

  B Listen and read.

Ashley: Hello, Ed. It's Ashley. What's the date today?
Ed: It's March 2nd.
Ashley: Well, what day is today? Is it a special day?
Ed: It's Wednesday.
Ashley: Wednesday, March 2nd?
Ed: Yes, that's right. Oh! Happy birthday, Ashley!

C Listen again and repeat.

D Work with a partner. Practice the conversation. Talk about today.

A: What's the _____ today?
B: It's _____.
A: What _____ is today?
B: It's _____.
A: _____, _____?
B: Yes, that's right.

✔ Ask for and give dates; interpret dates; take phone messages

2 Practice taking phone messages

  A Listen to the phone messages. Which call is in the evening?

B Listen again. Then complete the phone messages.

1

phone messages

Date:	10/5
Time:	3:00
From:	Tim
Phone number:	555-9241

Please call

2

phone messages

Date:	
Time:	
From:	Jackie
Phone number:	

Happy Birthday!

3

phone messages

Date:	
Time:	
From:	
Phone number:	

3 Practice your pronunciation

 A Listen and repeat the numbers in the chart.

-st	-nd	-rd	-th
first	second	third	fourth
twenty-first	twenty-second	twenty-third	twenty-fourth

  B Listen and circle *a* or *b*.

1. a. 1st
   b. 3rd
2. a. 23rd
   b. 26th
3. a. 7th
   b. 2nd
4. a. 4th
   b. 14th
5. a. 1st
   b. 21st
6. a. 3rd
   b. 23rd

C Work with a partner. Look at the calendar on page 34.
Partner A: Say a date. Partner B: Point to the date on the calendar.

4 Real-life math

Complete the sentences about Julie.

The date is March 10th.

Julie's birthday is on March 23rd.

Her birthday is _____ days from today.

Julie

TEST YOURSELF ✔

Tell a partner the names and birthdays of 3 friends or family members.
Write your partner's information.

1 Get ready to read

A Look at the pictures. Read the words.

① adult children

② large family

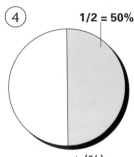
③ small family

④ 1/2 = 50%
percent (%)

B Work with classmates. Answer the questions.

1. How many children are in a large family?
2. How many children are in a small family?

2 Read about U.S. families

A Read the article.

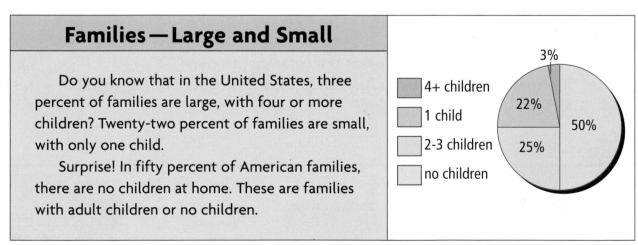

Families—Large and Small

Do you know that in the United States, three percent of families are large, with four or more children? Twenty-two percent of families are small, with only one child.

Surprise! In fifty percent of American families, there are no children at home. These are families with adult children or no children.

4+ children
1 child
2-3 children
no children

3%
22%
50%
25%

Source: *U.S. Census Bureau*

STUDENT AUDIO

B Listen and read the article again.

C Complete the sentences. Use the words in the box.

at home	~~large~~	small	families

1. Three percent of families in the U.S. are _large_____.
2. Twenty-two percent of families in the U.S. are _____.
3. In fifty percent of families, there are no children _____.
4. In twenty-five percent of _____, there are two or three children.

D Match the letters in the chart with the sentences. Look at the article in 2A for help.

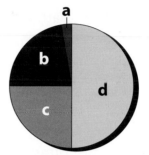

_b__ 1. families with one child

_____ 2. families with two or three children

_____ 3. families with four or more children

_____ 4. families with no children at home

3 Think about family size

A Think about your family. Answer the questions.

1. How many children are there in your home? _____
2. How many adults are there in your home? _____
3. Is your family large or small? _____

B Work with your classmates. Complete the chart.

	Number of children at home			
	1 child	2–3 children	4 or more children	no children
Number of classmates with:				

C Talk about the answers in the chart with your class.

Five people have one child.

BRING IT TO LIFE

Find pictures of families in newspapers, in magazines, or on the Internet. Bring the pictures to class. Talk about the pictures with your classmates.

1 Grammar

A Complete the sentences. Use *a* or *an*.

1. It's _a_ new computer.
2. It's ____ old computer.
3. She's ____ attractive child.
4. He's ____ tall man.
5. It's ____ easy exercise.
6. It's ____ difficult exercise.

new

old

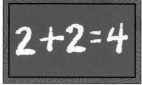

easy

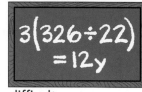

difficult

B Match the questions with the answers.

_c_ 1. What color are Mr. Smith's eyes?
____ 2. What color are his mother's eyes?
____ 3. What is your cousin's name?
____ 4. What time is your class?
____ 5. What time is her brother's class?
____ 6. What color is Marta's hair?

a. Her name is Jan.
b. My class is at 8:00.
c. His eyes are brown.
d. His class is at 10:00.
e. Her hair is brown.
f. Her eyes are blue.

C Work with a partner. Complete the chart. Then say the dates.

11/2	November 2nd
1/11	January 11th
6/3	
	October 1st

D Complete the story. Use the words in the box.

a	are	her	is	our	an	he	his	~~my~~	~~she~~

___My___ name is Jack. Dora is my wife. ___She___ is _____ attractive
      1   2   3
woman. Her eyes _____ green. _____ hair is black. _____ son's
                      4   5   6
name _____ Chris. _____ hair and eyes are brown. _____ is
           7   8   9
_____ good little boy.
     10

2 Group work

A Work with 2–3 classmates. Write 5 sentences about the family on page 29. Talk about the sentences with your class.

His name is Hector. He is Eric's uncle.

B Interview 3 classmates. Write their answers in your notebook.

ASK OR SAY:

1. Name a friend or family member.
2. What color is his or her hair?
3. What color are his or her eyes?

> Classmate–Alan
> 1. Raisa–sister
> 2. Her hair is red.
> 3. Her eyes are green.

C Talk about the answers with your class.

PROBLEM SOLVING

A Listen and read about Miguel. What is the problem?

Today is Miguel's first day of school. This is his new student ID card. Miguel is not happy with the card. There's a problem.

STUDENT ID CARD

Miguel Ramirez
123 First Street
Big City, CA 91100

Eyes: brown
Hair: blond
Date of birth: 11/09/82

Miguel Ramirez

B Work with your classmates. Answer the question. (More than one answer is possible.)

What can Miguel do?
  a. Go to the school office.
  b. Tell the teacher.
  c. Say nothing about it.
  d. Other: _____.

At Home

FOCUS ON
- places and things in the home
- things to do at home
- the present continuous
- paying bills
- addressing an envelope

LESSON **1** Vocabulary

1 Learn about places in the home

A Look at the picture. Name the colors.

 B Listen and look at the picture.

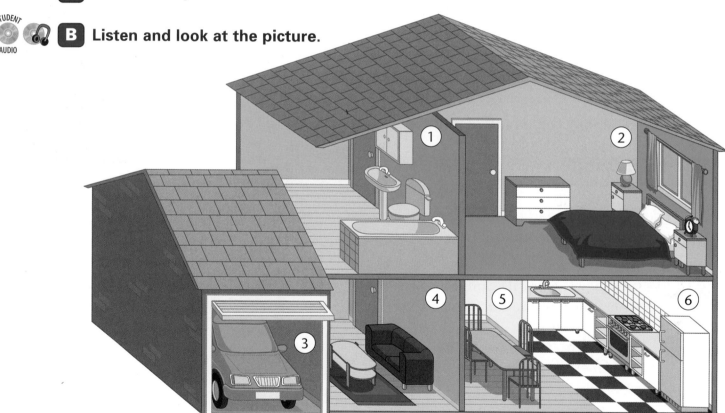

 C Listen and repeat the words.

1. bathroom	3. garage	5. dining area
2. bedroom	4. living room	6. kitchen

D Look at the picture. Complete the sentences.

1. The _____kitchen_____ is white.
2. The _____ is pink.
3. The _____ is green.
4. The _____ is gray.
5. The _____ is yellow.
6. The _____ is blue.

☑ Identify rooms in the home, furniture, and appliances

2 Talk about things in the home

A Work with your classmates. Match the words with the picture.

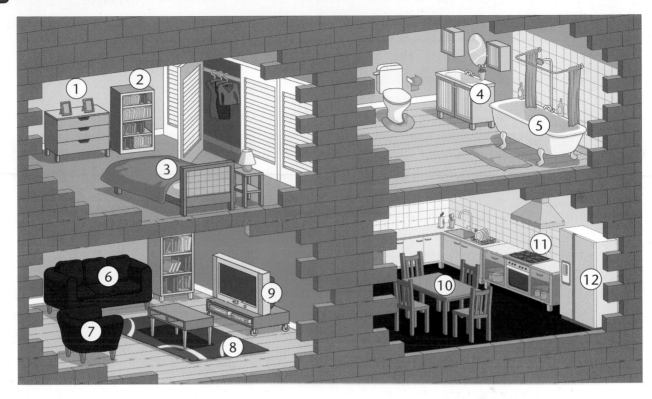

____	bathtub	____	chair	____	rug	____	stove
____	bed	_1_	dresser	____	sink	____	table
____	bookcase	____	refrigerator	____	sofa	____	TV (television)

B Listen and check your answers. Then practice the words with a partner.

C Cross out (X) the thing that is NOT usually in these rooms.

1. living room: sofa   TV   si~~nk~~
2. bedroom: dresser   stove   bed
3. kitchen: stove   refrigerator   bookcase
4. bathroom: bed   sink   bathtub

D Work with a partner. Ask and answer questions. Use the picture in 2A.

A: Where is the sofa?   A: Is the stove in the living room?
B: It's in the living room.   B: No, it isn't. It's in the kitchen.

TEST YOURSELF ✔

Close your book. Write 4 places and 6 things in the home. Check your spelling in a dictionary.

1 Read about things to do at home

  A Look at the pictures. Listen.

Sunday at Our Place

 B Listen again. Read the sentences.

1. My roommates and I go to Lake City College. We are at home today.
2. Robert is in the yard. He's cutting the grass.
3. Simon is watching TV in the living room.
4. Julio and Luis are in the bedroom. They are playing a video game.
5. And me? I'm cooking dinner and listening to music with my friend.
6. Sundays are great at our place.

C Check your understanding. Mark the sentences T (true) or F (false).

___T___ 1. Robert is in the yard.

___F___ 2. Simon is cooking in the kitchen.

___T___ 3. Julio and Luis are in the bedroom.

___F___ 4. Robert is studying.

___F___ 5. My friend and I are listening to music in the living room.

Pumpkin

2 Write about your home

A Look at the pictures on page 42. In your notebook, draw yourself and your family or friends in the rooms of your home.

B Use your picture to write your story.

My _____ and I are at home.

I am in the _____.

_____ is in the _____.

It's a _____ day at our home.

Need help?

It's a _____ day.
   good
   great
   special
   nice
   quiet

C Read your story to a partner.

3 Talk about your home

A Listen and look at the pictures.

Singular	
Near	this
Far	that

Plural	
Near	these
Far	those

B Study the charts and the pictures in 3A. Complete the sentences.

1. _This_ is a small TV.
2. _____ is a large TV.
3. _____ are brown chairs.
4. _____ are green chairs.

C Draw your home on the board. Ask and answer questions with your classmates.

A: *What's that?*
B: *This is my kitchen.*

A: *What are those?*
B: *These are my chairs.*

TEST YOURSELF ✓

Close your book. Write 3 sentences about things in your home.
   My sofa is in the living room.

1 Learn the present continuous

A Look at the pictures. Read the sentences. Who is working?

Tina is cleaning her home.

Mark is washing the windows.

Jean and Pam are eating lunch.

B Study the charts. Complete the sentences below.

THE PRESENT CONTINUOUS

Statements		
I	am	
You	are	eating.
He She It	is	

We		
You	are	eating.
They		

Contractions
I am = I'm
I'm eating.
We are = We're
We're eating.

1. I _____ eating.

2. They are _____ .

Negative statements		
I	am not	
You	are not	eating.
He She It	is not	

We		
You	are not	eating.
They		

Contractions
is not = isn't
He isn't eating.
are not = aren't
They aren't eating.

3. He _____ not eating.

4. We are _____ eating.

C Look at the pictures. Complete the sentences.

1. He _____is mopping_____ the floor.

2. She _____ the rug.

3. They _____ the furniture.

4. The cat _____ on the rug.

D Read the sentences to a partner.

mopping   vacuuming   dusting   sleeping

2 Ask and answer information questions

A Study the chart. Listen and repeat the questions and answers.

Information questions and answers	
A: What are you doing? **B:** I'm studying.	**A:** What are you doing? **B:** We're studying.
A: What is he doing? **B:** He's studying.	**A:** What are they doing? **B:** They're studying.

B Match the questions with the answers.

_c_ 1. What are Jean and Pam doing?

____ 2. What is Tina doing?

____ 3. What is Mark doing?

____ 4. What is the cat doing?

____ 5. What are you doing?

a. I'm studying.

b. It's sleeping.

c. They're eating.

d. He's washing the windows.

e. She's cleaning.

C Work with a partner. Complete the sentences with the words in the box.

am writing	is reading	is playing	are listening	are studying	is sleeping

1. **A:** What is Maria doing?

   B: She _____is reading_____ a book.

2. **A:** What are Janet and Nancy doing?

   B: They _____ to music.

3. **A:** What is Neil doing?

   B: He _____ a video game.

4. **A:** What are you doing?

   B: I _____ sentences.

5. **A:** What is the cat doing?

   B: It _____.

6. **A:** What am I doing?

   B: You _____ English.

3 Practice the present continuous

Work with your classmates. Follow the directions.

Student A: Act out an activity in the box. Don't talk.

Classmates: Guess the activity.

mopping	dusting	cooking	sleeping	vacuuming	studying	eating

TEST YOURSELF ✔

Close your book. Write the answers to the questions: What are you doing?
What is your teacher doing? What are you and your classmates studying?

LESSON 4 — Everyday conversation

1 Learn about utility bills

A Look at the utility bills. Complete the sentences below with the due dates.

Acme Electric Company

PAYMENT DUE
DATE:

10/01

electric bill

Atlantic Phone Service

PAYMENT DUE
DATE:

10/01

phone bill

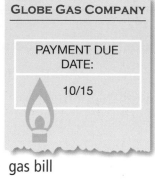

GLOBE GAS COMPANY

PAYMENT DUE
DATE:

10/15

gas bill

West Water Company

PAYMENT DUE
DATE:

10/15

water bill

1. Pay the electric bill and phone bill by _____.
2. Pay the gas bill and water bill by _____.

B Listen and write the totals for the utility bills.

1. The gas bill total is $ ___17.00___.   3. The electric bill total is $ _____.
2. The phone bill total is $ _____.   4. The water bill total is $ _____.

C Listen and read.

A: Can you help me?
B: Sure. What are you doing?
A: I'm writing a note to my roommate. He's not here.
B: OK. Read the note to me.
A: Please pay the gas bill. Tomorrow is the 31st.
B: That sounds good to me.

D Listen again and repeat.

E Work with a partner. Practice the conversation. Use your own information.

A: Can you help me?
B: Sure. What are you _____?
A: I'm writing a note to _____. _____ not here.
B: OK. Read the note to me.
A: Please pay the _____. Tomorrow is the _____.
B: That sounds good to me.

☑ Talk about utility bill due dates and write a short note

2 Learn subject and object pronouns

A Look at the pictures. Read the sentences.

1. <u>Joe</u> is talking to <u>Mary</u>.
   <u>He</u> is talking to <u>her</u>.

2. <u>Mary</u> is listening to <u>Joe</u>.
   <u>She</u> is listening to <u>him</u>.

3. <u>Mary</u> is paying <u>the bill</u>.
   <u>She</u> is paying <u>it</u>.

Please pay the phone bill today.

B Study the charts.

Subject pronouns	Object pronouns	Subject pronouns	Object pronouns
I	me	we	us
you	you	you	you
he	him	they	them
she	her		
it	it		

C Change the sentences. Use the pronouns in the chart.

1. <u>Martin</u> is writing to <u>Sara</u>. <u>He is writing to her.</u>

2. <u>Jean and Pat</u> are listening to <u>Mark</u>. _____

3. <u>Tina</u> is talking to <u>you and me</u>. _____

4. <u>You and I</u> are listening to <u>our teacher</u>. _____

5. <u>My sister</u> is talking to <u>Simon and Jack</u>. _____

6. <u>I</u> am looking at <u>my book</u>. _____

3 Real-life math

Look at exercise 1B. Add the utility bills. Complete the sentences.

1. The total for the electric bill and the phone bill is $_____.
2. The total for the gas bill and water bill is $_____.
3. The total for all of the utility bills is $_____.

TEST YOURSELF ✔

Write a note to a friend about a utility bill. Read the note to a partner.
Listen to your partner's note.

1 Get ready to read

A Look at the pictures. Read the words. What are the people doing?

   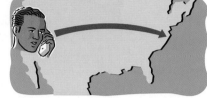   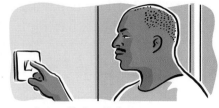

taking a shower   calling long distance   turning off the lights

B Think about the questions. Check (✔) your answers.

1. How long are your showers?
   - ☐ five minutes   ☐ fifteen minutes
   - ☐ ten minutes   ☐ twenty minutes

2. How long are your phone calls?
   - ☐ five minutes   ☐ twenty minutes
   - ☐ ten minutes   ☐ one hour

2 Read about saving money

A Read the website.

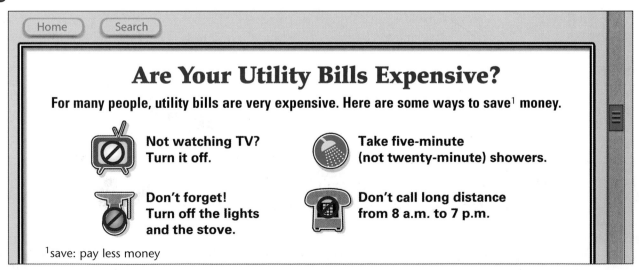

Source: *Oregon Department of Energy*

B Listen and read the website again.

STUDENT AUDIO

C Mark the sentences T (true) or F (false).

_____ 1. Save money. Turn the TV off.

_____ 2. Save money. Take twenty-minute showers.

_____ 3. Save money. Call long distance from 8 a.m. to 7 p.m.

D Circle the correct words.

1. Some utility bills are (expensive / five-minute).
2. You can (save / turn off) money on your bills.
3. Don't forget! Turn off the (phone / lights).

3 Addressing an envelope

A Look at the envelope. What kind of utility bill is this?

B Look at the envelope. Circle the correct answers.

1. Who is paying the bill?
   a. Atlantic Phone Services
   b. Mavis Clark
   c. Greene, Texas

2. What is the city in the mailing address?
   a. Greene
   b. Clark
   c. Dallas

C Think about the questions. Talk about the answers with your class.

1. When do you pay your utility bills?
2. Why is a return address on an envelope important?

BRING IT TO LIFE

Look at a utility bill at home. Address an envelope for the bill or address an envelope for the phone company in 3A. Bring the envelope to class.

1 Grammar

A Circle the correct words.

1. **A:** (Is / Are) Ed and Sue eating?
   B: Yes, (we / they) are.
2. **A:** Is Tom (cooking / cook)?
   B: No, he (isn't / aren't).
3. **A:** Is the (rug / girl) sleeping?
   B: No, (it / she) isn't.
4. **A:** (Is / Are) you and Sam studying?
   B: Yes, (I / we) are.

> **Grammar note**
>
> *Yes/No questions and answers*
>
> **A:** Are you working?
> **B:** Yes, I am. *or*
>   No, I'm not.
>
> **A:** Is Mark cooking?
> **B:** Yes, he is. *or*
>   No, he isn't.
>
> **A:** Are you working?
> **B:** Yes, we are. *or*
>   No, we aren't.
>
> **A:** Are they playing?
> **B:** Yes, they are. *or*
>   No, they aren't.

B Write answers for these questions.

1. Are you studying English? <u>Yes, I am.</u>
2. Are you mopping the floor? _____
3. Is your teacher eating lunch? _____
4. Are your classmates writing the answers? _____
5. Are you working with a partner? _____

C Write new sentences. Use object pronouns.

1. Janet is talking to <u>Joe</u>.
   <u>Janet is talking to him.</u>
2. Jeff is writing to <u>Maria</u>.
   _____
3. Paul is listening to <u>his friends</u>.
   _____
4. Ingrid is talking to <u>Jane and me</u>.
   _____

D Match the questions with the answers.

<u>b</u> 1. Where is she?   a. Yes, he is.
____ 2. What's he doing?   b. She's in the living room.
____ 3. Is he studying English?   c. No, they aren't.
____ 4. What time is it?   d. He's studying.
____ 5. Are Mr. and Mrs. Li at home? e. It's 6:00.

2 Group work

A Work with 2–3 classmates. Write 5 questions and answers about the picture on page 41. Talk about the sentences with your class.

A: *Where is the sofa?*
B: *It's in the living room.*

A: *Is the sink in the kitchen?*
B: *Yes, it is.*

B Interview 3 classmates. Write their answers in your notebook.

SAY:

1. Tell me where you study.
2. Tell me where you eat.
3. Tell me where you pay your bills.

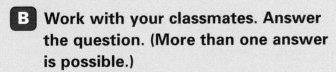

Classmate—Nancy
1. in the living room
2. in the kitchen
3. in the living room

C Talk about the answers with your class.

PROBLEM SOLVING

A Listen and read about Mrs. Simms. What is the problem?

The Simms family is at home today. Mrs. Simms is cleaning the house. Her son, Jack, is listening to music. Her daughters, Judy and Joni, are watching TV. Mrs. Simms is tired. She's doing all the work.

B Work with your classmates. Answer the question. (More than one answer is possible.)

What can Mrs. Simms do?
   a. Play video games.
   b. Tell the children to help.
   c. Pay the children to help.
   d. Other: _____

In the Neighborhood

FOCUS ON
- places and transportation
- describing locations
- *there is/there are*
- maps and directions
- preparing for emergencies

LESSON **1** Vocabulary

1 Learn neighborhood words

A Look at the map. Say the names of the streets.

 B Listen and look at the map.

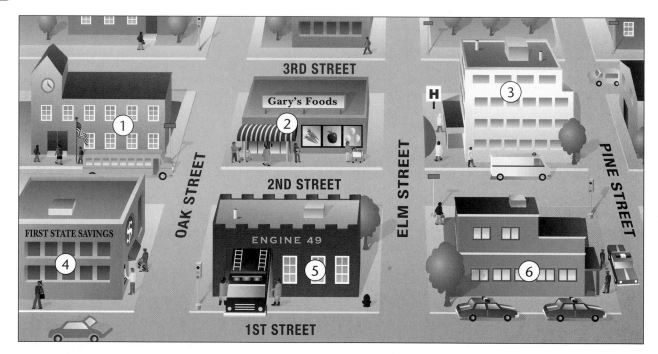

 C Listen and repeat the words.

1. school	3. hospital	5. fire station
2. supermarket	4. bank	6. police station

D Look at the map. Complete the sentences.

1. The ___supermarket___ is on 2nd Street.
2. The _____ is on Elm Street.
3. The _____ is on 1st Street.
4. The _____ is on Oak Street.
5. The _____ is on Pine Street.
6. The _____ is on 2nd Street.

☑ Identify common neighborhood places and modes of transportation

2 Talk about transportation and places

A Work with your classmates. Match the words with the picture.

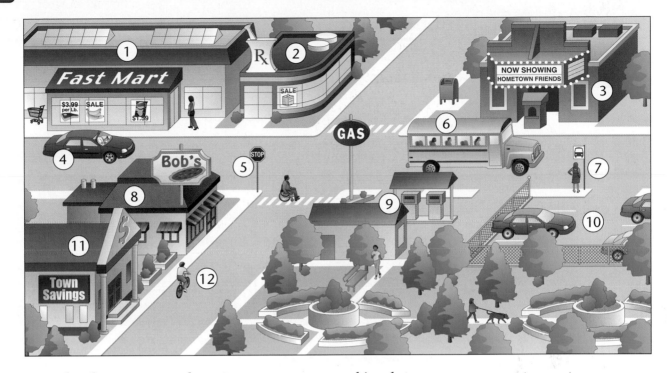

bank	___ bus stop	___ parking lot	___ restaurant
bicycle	car	movie theater	stop sign
___ bus	___ gas station	___ pharmacy	_1_ supermarket

B Listen and check your answers. Then practice the words with a partner.

C Look at the picture in 2A. Circle the correct words.

1. The boy is riding ((a bicycle) / a car).
2. The children are riding (a bicycle / the bus).
3. The woman is going to (the pharmacy / the supermarket).
4. The man is driving (a car / a bicycle).
5. The girl is standing at (the bus stop / the stop sign).

D Work with a partner. Practice the conversations. Use the pictures in 1A and 2A.

A: Where is the school?

B: It's on 2nd Street.

A: What's the woman doing?

B: She's going to the supermarket.

TEST YOURSELF ✓

Close your book. Write 5 neighborhood places and 3 transportation words. Check your spelling in a dictionary.

1 Read about a neighborhood

 A **Look at the pictures. Listen.**

My Neighborhood

My apartment   My favorite movie theater   My supermarket   Me

 B **Listen again. Read the sentences.**

1. Let me tell you about my new neighborhood.
2. My apartment building is on 6th Street. It's next to a little library.
3. There is a big park behind the library.
4. My favorite movie theater is near my home. It's across from the post office.
5. My supermarket is on Main Street between the bank and the clinic.
6. There is a bus stop in front of my apartment. That's me. I'm waiting for the bus.

next to   behind   in front of   across from   between

C **Check your understanding. Mark the sentences T (true) or F (false).**

_T_ 1. His apartment is next to the library.

____ 2. There is a bank behind the library.

____ 3. The supermarket is on Main Street.

____ 4. The bus stop is in front of the clinic.

2 Write about your neighborhood

A Write about your neighborhood. Complete the sentences.

Let me tell you about my neighborhood.

My apartment/house is across from _____.

There is a/an _____ next to my home.

There is a/an _____ behind my home.

B Read your sentences to a partner.

3 Talk about locations

A Listen to the directions. Label the map with the words in the box.

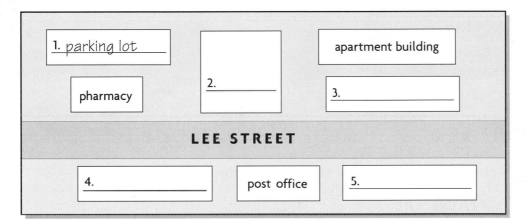

1. parking lot		apartment building
pharmacy	2.	3.

LEE STREET

4.	post office	5.

clinic
fire station
hospital
supermarket
~~parking lot~~

B Look at the map. Circle the correct word.

1. The parking lot is (between / (behind)) the pharmacy.
2. The supermarket is (in front of / on) the apartment building.
3. The pharmacy is (in front of / across from) the hospital.
4. The clinic is (across from / next to) the supermarket.
5. The post office is (between / behind) the hospital and the fire station.

C Listen. Then practice the conversations with a partner. Use your own information.

A: Where is your favorite supermarket?

B: It's on Main Street next to the bank.

A: Where is your favorite restaurant?

B: It's on 1st Street across from the park.

TEST YOURSELF ✔

Close your book. Ask a partner to give the location of 3 places in his or her neighborhood. Write what you hear.

1 Learn *There is* and *There are*

A **Listen and look at the picture. Read the story. Find Dave in the picture.**

I'm Dave. I live on 4th Street. There are two restaurants on my street. One restaurant is next to my apartment building. There is a nice park across the street. Right now I'm sitting on a bench in the park. It's my favorite place to have lunch.

B **Study the charts. Complete the sentences below.**

THERE IS / THERE ARE

Statements
There is a supermarket on 4th Street. There are two restaurants.

Negative statements
There isn't a post office. There aren't any schools.

1. There _____ a supermarket on 4th Street.

2. There _____ two restaurants.

3. There _____ a post office.

4. There _____ any schools.

C **Look at the picture in 1A. Change the sentences from false to true.**

1. There is one restaurant. <u>There are two restaurants.</u>

2. There's a movie theater. _____

3. There are two mailboxes. _____

4. There are two gas stations. _____

D **Work with a partner. Use *There is* and *There are* to talk about your classroom.**

There are ten students in the classroom. There's a green notebook on my desk.

2 Ask and answer *Yes/No* questions with *there is* and *there are*

A Study the chart. Listen and repeat the questions and answers.

Yes/No questions and answers with *there is* and *there are*	
A: Is there a park on 4th Street? **B:** Yes, there is.	**A:** Are there any restaurants on 4th Street? **B:** Yes, there are.
A: Is there a clinic on 4th Street? **B:** No, there isn't.	**A:** Are there any schools on 4th Street? **B:** No, there aren't.

B Write the questions. Use *Is there* or *Are there*.

1. **A:** <u>Is there a park on 4th Street?</u>

   B: Yes, there's a park on 4th Street.

2. **A:** _____

   B: Yes, there is. There's a supermarket on 4th Street.

3. **A:** _____

   B: Yes, there are many people in the park.

4. **A:** _____

   B: No, there isn't. There isn't a pharmacy on 4th Street.

3 Practice *Yes/No* questions with *there is* and *there are*

A Think about your neighborhood. Complete the questions in the chart. Then write the answers.

Questions	My answers	My partner's answers
1. <u>Is there</u> a library?		
2. _____ a good restaurant?		
3. _____ any bus stops?		

B Interview a partner. Write your partner's answers in the chart.

C Talk about the answers in the chart with your class.

There's a library in my neighborhood. There isn't a library in Ivan's neighborhood.

TEST YOURSELF ✔

Close your book. Write 3 sentences about your school's neighborhood.
Use *there is* and *there are*.

1 Learn directions

A Look at the pictures. Read the directions.

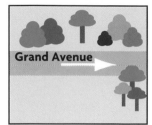

Grand Avenue

Go straight.

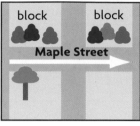

block   block

Maple Street

Go two blocks.

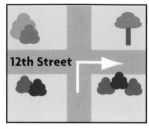

12th Street

Turn right.

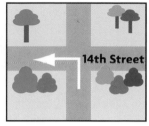

14th Street

Turn left.

B Listen. Complete the directions to the clinic.

1. Go _straight_ on Grand Avenue.

2. Turn _____ on 12th Street.

3. Go two _____ on Maple Street.

4. Turn _____ on 14th Street.

5. It's _____ the park.

6. It's _____ to the pharmacy.

C Listen and read.

A: Excuse me. Is there a bank near here?

B: Yes, there is. Go one block on Main Street and turn left on 6th Avenue. The bank is on the corner, next to the clinic.

A: Thanks for your help.

B: No problem. Have a nice day.

D Listen again and repeat each line.

E Work with a partner. Practice the conversation. Use the map.

A: Excuse me. Is there a _____ near here?

B: Yes, there is. Go _____ on _____ and turn _____ on _____. It's on the corner, next to the _____.

A: Thanks for your help.

B: No problem. Have a nice day.

PINE

Gas station

Supermarket

Pharmacy

Park

MAPLE

5TH

6TH

Bank

Clinic

MAIN

● **You are here.**

☑ Ask for, give, and follow directions; use a simple map

2 Practice your pronunciation

A **Listen to the sentences. Listen for the stressed words.**

1. The **police** **station** is in **front** of the **park**.
2. It's **across** from the **library**.
3. There's a **restaurant** **next** to the **movie** **theater**.
4. It's **behind** the **parking** **lot**.

B **Listen and underline the stressed words. Read the sentences to a partner.**

1. There's a <u>park</u> <u>behind</u> the <u>fire</u> <u>station</u>.
2. The bank is next to the post office.
3. There are two restaurants on the street.
4. The bus stop is in front of the restaurant.

3 Real-life math

A **Complete the sentences. How far is it?**

1. It's ___235___ miles* from Miami to Orlando.
2. It's _____ miles from Orlando to Tampa.
3. It's _____ miles from Tampa to Daytona Beach.
4. It's _____ miles from Miami to Daytona Beach.

*1 mile = 1.61 kilometers

B **Work with a partner. Make sentences about the map.**

It's _____ miles from _____
to _____.

TEST YOURSELF ✔

Work with a partner. Partner A: Ask for directions to a place near
your school. Partner B: Give the directions. Then change roles.

1 Get ready to read

A Look at the pictures. Read the words.

Home Emergencies

1

Fire

2

Power outage

3

Accident

B Work with your classmates. Make a list of other home emergencies. Ask your teacher for the words you need in English, or use a dictionary.

2 Read about home emergencies

A Read the poster.

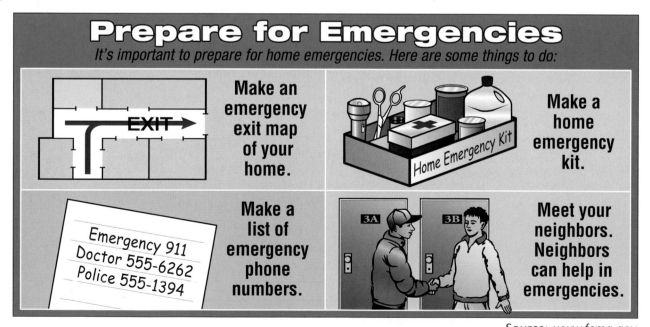

Prepare for Emergencies

It's important to prepare for home emergencies. Here are some things to do:

Make an emergency exit map of your home.

Make a home emergency kit.

Home Emergency Kit

Make a list of emergency phone numbers.

Emergency 911
Doctor 555-6262
Police 555-1394

Meet your neighbors. Neighbors can help in emergencies.

Source: www.fema.gov

STUDENT AUDIO

B Listen and read the poster again.

C Mark the sentences T (true) or F (false).

To prepare for home emergencies:

___T___ 1. Make an exit map for your home.

_____ 2. Make an emergency kit for your teacher.

_____ 3. Call the doctor.

_____ 4. Make a list of emergency phone numbers.

D Complete the sentences. Use the words in the box.

exit	~~prepare~~	neighbors	kit

1. It's important to ___prepare___ for home emergencies.

2. Make an emergency _____ map.

3. Make a home emergency _____.

4. Meet your _____.

3 Read an emergency exit map

A Look at the emergency exit map. Answer the questions below.

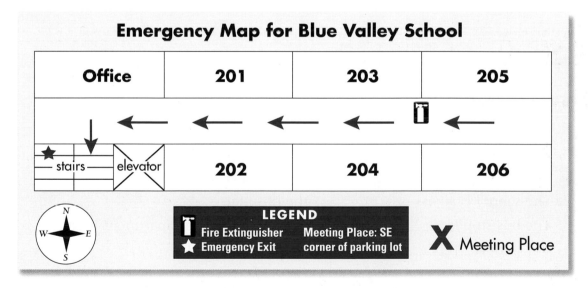

1. Is there an emergency exit in the building? _____

2. Are there any fire extinguishers in the classrooms? _____

B Work with a your classmates. Draw an emergency exit map for your classroom.

BRING IT TO LIFE

Work with your family or roommates at home. Make a home emergency exit map. Bring your map to class.

1 Grammar

A Complete the questions. Then answer the questions. Use your own information.

1. A: How many parks are ___there___ near your school?

   B: There _____ near our school.

2. A: How many good restaurants _____ there near your school?

   B: There _____ near our school.

3. A: How _____ students are there in class today?

   B: _____ in class today.

4. A: _____ many computers are there in your classroom?

   B: There _____ in my classroom.

5. A: How _____ books are there on your desk?

   B: There _____ on my desk.

> **Grammar note**
>
> *How many?*
> A: How many banks are there on Elm Street?
> B: There is one bank on Elm Street.
> A: How many people are there in the park?
> B: There are four people in the park.

B Complete the sentences. Use the words in the box.

| ~~to~~ | from | of | in | on |

1. The parking lot is next _____to_____ the supermarket.
2. The school is across _____ the hospital.
3. The bus stop is _____ front _____ the apartment building.
4. The park is _____ the corner.

C Unscramble the sentences.

1. a / theater / on / 1st / movie / There's / Avenue _There's a movie theater on 1st Avenue_.
2. on / the / The / is / park / corner _____.
3. here / Is / near / there / clinic / a _____?
4. thc / pcople / many / in / How / are / park _____?
5. street / two / There / gas / my / stations / are / on _____.

2 Group work

A Work with 2–3 classmates. Write 5 questions about the pictures on page 53. Talk about the questions with your class.

Where is the supermarket?
Is there a bus on the street?

B Interview 3 classmates. Write their answers in your notebook.

ASK:

1. Is there a gas station on your street?
2. Is there a new movie theater in your neighborhood?
3. Are there any schools in your neighborhood?
4. How many supermarkets are there in your neighborhood?

> *Classmate—Malaya*
> *1. Yes, there is.*
> *2. No, there isn't.*
> *3. Yes, there are.*
> *4. There are two supermarkets.*

C Talk about the answers with your class.

PROBLEM SOLVING

A Listen and read about Jim. What is his problem?

Jim is new in the neighborhood. His apartment is on Green Street. He is looking for the supermarket, but there's a problem with the directions. Jim is confused.

B Work with your classmates. Answer the question. (More than one answer is possible.)

What can Jim do?
  a. Go to a restaurant and eat.
  b. Ask a neighbor for help.
  c. Go home.
  d. Other: _____

Daily Routines

FOCUS ON

- everyday activities
- schedules
- the simple present
- office machines and equipment
- daily routines

LESSON **1** Vocabulary

1 Learn everyday activity words

A Look at the pictures. Say the times.

B Listen and look at the pictures.

1 7:00 a.m.

2 7:15 a.m.

3 7:30 a.m.

4 5:30 p.m.

5 6:00 p.m.

6 11:00 p.m.

C Listen and repeat the words.

1. get up   3. eat breakfast   5. make dinner
2. get dressed   4. come home   6. go to bed

D Look at the pictures. Complete the sentences.

1. They _____go to bed_____ at 11:00 p.m.   4. They _____ at 7:00 a.m.
2. They _____ at 7:15 a.m.   5. They _____ at 5:30 p.m.
3. They _____ at 6:00 p.m.   6. They _____ at 7:30 a.m.

☑ **Identify and discuss daily routines**

2 Talk about a school day

A Work with your classmates. Match the words with the pictures.

____ do homework	____ have lunch	____ take a shower
____ do housework	____ go to bed	_1_ walk to school
____ drink coffee	____ ride the bus	____ work

B Listen and check your answers. Then practice the words with a partner.

C Complete the sentences. Use the words in the box. Use your own information to write the times.

go	have	~~take~~	do	get	come

1. I ____take____ a shower at _____.
2. I _____ dressed at _____.
3. I _____ to bed at _____.
4. I _____ home at _____.
5. I _____ lunch at _____.
6. I _____ homework at _____.

D Read your sentences to a partner.

TEST YOURSELF ✔

Close your book. Write the activities you do in the morning, afternoon, and evening. Check your spelling in a dictionary.

1 Read about a work schedule

A **Look at the pictures. Listen.**

Good morning.
Doctor's office.

B **Listen again. Read the sentences.**

1. My name is Tina Aziz. I work in a doctor's office.
2. This is my work schedule. I work from 9 a.m. to 5 p.m., Monday to Thursday.
3. I turn on the computer and copy machine at 9:00. I answer the phone all day.
4. At noon, I meet my friend. We have lunch and talk.
5. On Fridays, I don't work. I relax. I take my kids to the park.
6. I like my job and my schedule a lot, but Friday is my favorite day.

C **Check your understanding. Circle _a_ or _b_.**

1. Tina works ____.
   a. four days a week
   b. on Saturday

2. She answers the phone ____.
   a. at 9 a.m.
   b. all day

3. Tina and her friend have lunch ____.
   a. at 11 a.m.
   b. at 12 p.m.

4. She likes her job ____.
   a. a lot
   b. a little

2 Write about your schedule

A Write about your schedule. Complete the sentences.

I go to school from _____ to _____ .

I study _____ at school.

On _____ , I relax.

I _____ .

Need help?

Ways to relax
go to the park
watch TV
listen to music
talk to friends and family
take a walk

B Read your story to a partner.

3 Talk about a work schedule

A Listen and check (✔) the activities you hear.

_____ 1. mop the floor

_____ 2. vacuum the rug

_____ 3. answer the phone

_____ 4. wash the windows

_____ 5. turn on the copy machine

_____ 6. help the manager

Mel at work

B Listen again. Complete Mel's work schedule.

MORNING 10 A.M.–12 P.M.	AFTERNOON 12 P.M.–3 P.M.
1. mop the floor	3. _____
2. _____	4. _____

C Listen and repeat.

A: I work on Saturday and Sunday. How about you?

B: I don't work.

A: I go to school from Monday to Friday. How about you?

B: I go to school on Monday and Wednesday.

D Work with a partner. Practice the conversation. Use your own information.

TEST YOURSELF ✔

Close your book. Listen to your partner's schedule for the week. Write the schedule you hear.

1 Learn the simple present

A Look at the pictures. Read the sentences. What time does she leave for work?

She exercises at 6:00 a.m.

She has breakfast at 7:15 a.m.

She brushes her teeth at 7:30 a.m.

She leaves the house at 8:00 a.m.

B Study the charts. Complete the sentences below.

THE SIMPLE PRESENT

Statements			
I You	exercise.	We You	exercise.
He She	exercise**s**.	They	

1. He _____. 2. We _____.

Negative statements					Contractions

I
You
	do not exercise.	We
		You
			do not exercise.		do not = don't
					    I don't exercise.
					does not = doesn't
					    He doesn't exercise.

He She	does not exercise.	They			

3. You _____ exercise. 4. They do not _____.

C Complete the sentences. Use the words in the box.

~~rides~~   gets   don't   doesn't

1. She _____rides_____ the bus every day.
2. He _____ up at 6 a.m.
3. She _____ drink coffee.
4. They _____ have breakfast every morning.

D Read the sentences to a partner.

2 Ask and answer information questions

A Study the chart. Work with a partner. Ask and answer the questions.

Information questions and answers	
A: When do you exercise? **B:** I exercise every day.	**A:** When does he exercise? **B:** He exercises every Saturday.
A: When does she exercise? **B:** She exercises at 6 a.m.	**A:** When do they exercise? **B:** They exercise in the evening.

B Circle the correct word in the questions. Complete the answers.

1. **A:** When (do / does) you get up?

   B: I ___get up___ at 6:30 a.m.

2. **A:** When (do / does) they study?

   B: They _____ every day.

3. **A:** When does (you / she) exercise?

   B: She _____ in the morning.

4. **A:** When (do / does) Joe work?

   B: He _____ every weekend*.

5. **A:** When does Ruby (cook / cooks)?

   B: She _____ every evening.

6. **A:** When (do / does) you study?

   B: I study _____.

*weekend = Saturday and Sunday

3 Practice questions about your day

A Write your answers in the chart.

Questions	My answers	My partner's answers
1. When do you get up?		
2. When do you leave the house?		
3. When do you come home?		
4. When do you make dinner?		

B Interview a partner. Write your partner's answers in the chart.

C Talk about the answers in the chart with your class.

I get up at 6 a.m. Ruby gets up at 7:30.

TEST YOURSELF ✔

Close your book. Write 3 activities you do every day and 3 activities you don't do every day.

1 Learn about office machines and equipment

A Look at the pictures. Read the sentences. Then answer the questions about your classroom.

(1)

Turn on the computer.
Push this button.

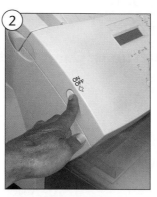

(2)

Turn off the printer.
Push this button.

(3)

Fill the copy machine.
Put the paper here.

(4)

Fill the stapler.
Put the staples here.

1. Is there a copy machine in your classroom?   <u>No, there isn't.</u>

2. Are there any computers?   _____

3. Is there a printer?   _____

4. How many staplers are there?   _____

B Listen and read.

A: Ms. Barns, can you help me?

B: Yes, Mr. Glenn.

A: How do I turn on the computer?

B: Push this button.

A: Thanks for your help, Ms. Barns.

B: That's my job, Mr. Glenn. That's my job.

C Listen again and repeat.

D Work with a partner. Practice the conversation. Use the information from 1A.

A: _____, can you help me?

B: Yes, _____.

A: How do I _____?

B: _____.

A: Thanks for your help.

☑ Identify office machines and follow operating instructions

E Listen and match. Write the number under the picture.

____   ____   1   ____

2 Practice your pronunciation

A Listen to the sentences.

"s"	"z"	"iz"
He helps customers.	He fills the stapler.	He closes the store.
She counts the money.	She cleans offices.	She washes windows.
It prints.	It copies.	It uses staples.

B Read the sentences in the chart.

C Work with a partner. Talk about Miguel's work routine.

He works at the supermarket. He opens the store.

TEST YOURSELF ✔

Work with a partner. Partner A: Ask for help with an office machine.
Partner B: Help your partner. Then change roles.

1 Get ready to read

A Look at the pictures. Read the words.

He sleeps <u>a little</u>.   He sleeps <u>a lot</u>.

B Think about your daily routine. Check (✔) the boxes.

	I work …	I study …	I sleep …	I relax …	I exercise …
a little					
a lot					

C Talk about your daily routine with your classmates. Use the chart.

I work a lot.

2 Read about daily routines in the U.S.

A Read the article.

WHERE DOES THE TIME GO?

Many people in the U.S. work a lot and relax a little. Here's what people say about their daily routines.

They sleep for seven or eight hours.

[1] get ready: the things you do before you leave home every day

They get ready[1] for work for one hour. They walk, drive, or ride to work for twenty-five minutes. They work for eight or nine hours. They do housework for one or two hours every day. Then they have free time. They relax for two or three hours. They read, spend time with family, or watch TV.

Where does the time go? Now you know!

B Listen and read the article again.

Source: *The NPD Group, Inc.*

C Mark the sentences T (true) or F (false).

__T__ 1. Many people do housework every day.

____ 2. People don't walk or drive to work.

____ 3. Many people get ready for work for two or three hours every day.

____ 4. Many people in the U.S. don't relax a lot.

D Complete the sentences. Use the words in the box.

do housework	relax	~~sleep~~	work

1. People _____ sleep _____ for seven or eight hours every day.
2. People _____ for eight or nine hours every day.
3. People _____ for two or three hours every day.
4. People _____ for one to two hours every day.

3 Read about housework

A Look at the graph. Complete the sentences.

1. _____ cook and clean the kitchen for seven hours every week.
2. Men work in the yard for _____ hours every week.

B Think about the graph. Talk about the answers with your class.

1. What kinds of housework do men do a lot? What do they do a little?
2. What kinds of housework do women do a lot? What do women do a little?

BRING IT TO LIFE

Find pictures of everyday activities. Look in newspapers, magazines, or on the Internet. Bring the pictures to class. Talk about them with your classmates.

1 Grammar

A Circle *a* or *b*.

1. I _____ lunch at noon.
   a. have
   b. has

2. Marvin _____ breakfast every day.
   a. have
   b. has

3. Kayla _____ have any free time today.
   a. don't
   b. doesn't

4. Lev and Min _____ have class on Saturday.
   a. don't
   b. doesn't

> **Grammar note**
>
> *have*
>
> I
> You } have free time.
> We } don't have free time.
> They
>
> He } has free time.
> She } doesn't have free time.

B Match the questions with the answers.

_b_ 1. When do they have lunch?

____ 2. Where do they eat dinner?

____ 3. When does John have lunch?

____ 4. When does Kyle make breakfast?

____ 5. Does Don eat breakfast?

a. He has lunch at noon.

b. They have lunch in the afternoon.

c. Yes, he does.

d. They eat at home.

e. He makes breakfast at 7 a.m.

C Write the questions. Use *When*.

1. A: _When does she walk to school?_

   B: She walks to school every afternoon.

2. A: _____

   B: I clean the kitchen every Saturday.

3. A: _____

   B: They go to the park every weekend.

4. A: _____

   B: He rides the bus every day.

5. A: _____

   B: We relax every weekend.

2 Group work

A Work with 2–3 classmates. Write 5 questions and answers about the pictures on page 65. Talk about the sentences with your class.

When does she walk to school?
She walks to school in the morning.

B Interview 3 classmates. Write their answers in your notebook.

ASK:

1. When do you get up?
2. When do you have lunch?
3. When do you relax with your family and friends?

Classmate—Lara
1. at 6 a.m.
2. in the afternoon
3. every evening

C Talk about the answers with your class.

PROBLEM SOLVING

A Listen and read about Nick. What is his problem?

Today is Nick's first day at his new job. He works at a bank. He answers the phones and works at a computer. Nick's manager says, "Make 100 copies and staple them for me." Nick doesn't understand the directions on the copy machine.

B Work with your classmates. Answer the question. (More than one answer is possible.)

What can Nick do?

   a. Ask another person to make the copies.
   b. Ask the manager for help.
   c. Open and close all the copy machine doors.
   d. Other: _____

C Work with your classmates. Make a list of things Nick can say.

Shop and Spend

FOCUS ON
- money and shopping
- clothing
- simple present *yes/no* questions
- expressing needs and wants
- ATMs and personal checks

LESSON **1** Vocabulary

1 Learn money words

A Look at the pictures. What's the total of the cash?

 B Listen and look at the pictures.

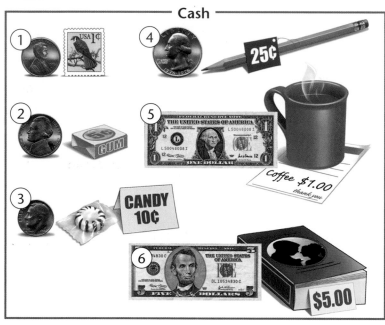

 C Listen and repeat the words.

1. penny   3. dime   5. one-dollar bill   7. check
2. nickel   4. quarter   6. five-dollar bill   8. money order

D Look at the pictures. Complete the sentences.

1. The pencil is 25¢. Pay with a _quarter_.
2. The gum is 5¢. Pay with a _____.
3. The candy is 10¢. Pay with a _____.
4. The stamp is 1¢. Pay with a _____.
5. The rent is $300. Pay with a _____.
6. The book is $5. Pay with a _____.
7. The gas bill is $45. Pay with a _____.
8. The coffee is $1. Pay with a _____.

☑ Count and use currency; identify clothing items

2 Talk about clothes

A Work with your classmates. Match the words with the picture.

____ blouse	<u>1</u> customer	____ pants	____ shoes	____ socks	____ tie
____ change	____ dress	____ shirt	____ skirt	____ suit	____ T-shirt

B Listen and check your answers. Then practice the words with a partner.

C Look at the picture. Match the questions with the answers.

<u>d</u> 1. How much is the dress?   a. $19.99

____ 2. What color are the shoes?   b. two

____ 3. How much is the shirt?   c. black

____ 4. How many customers are there?   d. $9.99

____ 5. How many people are working?   e. four

D Work with a partner. Ask and answer questions.
Use the pictures in 1A and 2A.

A: How much is the pencil?   A: How much are the pants?
B: It's 25¢.   B: They're $24.99.

TEST YOURSELF ✔

Close your book. Write 6 clothing words and 6 money words. Check your spelling in a dictionary.

1 Read about shopping at a mall

  A **Look at the pictures. Listen.**

May I help you?

 B **Listen again. Read the sentences.**

1. It's cold today. I need a new sweater. It's time to go to the mall!
2. I shop at Dan's Discount Store. The salespeople are friendly. The prices are good.
3. I want an inexpensive yellow sweater.
4. I don't like this one. It's yellow, but it's too expensive.
5. This sweater is perfect. It's beautiful, and it's on sale.
6. I usually pay with cash, but I have a new credit card. I'm using it today.

C **Check your understanding. Mark the sentences T (true) or F (false).**

___T___ 1. She's shopping at the mall.

_____ 2. The salespeople at Dan's are not friendly.

_____ 3. She wants a yellow sweater.

_____ 4. She has a new credit card.

2 Write about shopping

A Write about yourself. Complete the sentences.

I (like / don't like) the mall.

I shop at _____.

I need _____.

I want _____.

I usually pay _____.

> **Need help?**
>
> **Ways to pay**
> with cash
> with a check
> with a credit card

B Read your story to a partner.

3 Talk about what to wear

A Listen to John talk about his clothes. Write the words you hear.

1. _____
2. _____
3. sneakers

at home

4. hat
5. uniform
6. belt

at work

7. _____
8. _____
9. _____

on special occasions

B Work with a partner. Look at the pictures. Talk about what John likes to wear.

A: What does John wear at home?

B: He wears a T-shirt and jeans.

C Listen and repeat.

A: What do you wear at home?

B: At home, I wear a T-shirt and jeans.

D Work with a partner. Practice the conversation. Use your own information.

TEST YOURSELF ✔

Close your book. Write 3 sentences about what you wear at home, at work, and on special occasions.

1 Learn simple present *Yes/No* questions

A **Look at the pictures. Read the sentences. Who needs a jacket?**

Jim and Joe have new jackets.

Ann doesn't have a jacket.
She needs a jacket.

Mario has a jacket.
He wants a new jacket.

B **Study the charts. Complete the sentences below.**

SIMPLE PRESENT *YES/NO* QUESTIONS

Questions			
Do	I you we they	need	a jacket?
			jackets?
Does	he she		a jacket?

Answers						
Yes,	I you we they	do.	No,	I you we they	don't.
	he she	does.		he she	doesn't.

1. A: _____ Ann _____ a jacket?   2. A: Do Jim and Joe need _____?

   B: Yes, _____ does.   B: No, they _____.

C **Match the questions with the answers. Use the pictures in 1A.**

_a_ 1. Does Mario have a jacket?   a. Yes, he does.

___ 2. Do Jim and Joe need new jackets?   b. No, he doesn't.

___ 3. Does Mario need a jacket?   c. No, they don't.

___ 4. Does Ann have a jacket?   d. No, she doesn't.

D **Work with a partner. Ask and answer the questions. Look at the pictures in 1A.**

A: Does Ann want a jacket?

B: Yes, she does.

A: Do Jim and Joe need new jackets?

B: No, they don't.

✔ Ask and answer simple present *Yes/No* questions to describe needs

2 Ask and answer simple present *Yes/No* questions

A Complete the answers.

1. A: Does the store have a bathroom?

   B: No, _____ it doesn't _____.

2. A: Do the children have new jeans?

   B: Yes, _____.

3. A: Do Ben and Rosa have a new car?

   B: No, _____.

4. A: Does Sue want a sweater?

   B: Yes, _____.

B Write questions. Use *Do* or *Does.*

1. A: _Do you want new _____

   B: Yes, I do. I want r_____ suit.

2. A: _____

   B: Yes, they do. They _____ oes.

C Write about what you *have, need,* and *want.* Read your sent_____
a partner.

1. I _____ want _____ a new jacket.

2. I _ don't need _ a new car.

3. I _____ a dictionary.

4. I _____ a job.

5. I _____ brown shoe

6. I _____ a new ___

3 Practice simple present *Yes/No* questions

A Read the questions. Write your answers in the chart.

Questions	My answers	My partner's answers
1. Do you have new shoes?		
2. Do you need a sweater?		
3. Do you want new clothes?		

B Interview a partner. Write your partner's answers in the chart.

C Talk about the answers in the chart with your class.

Maria has new shoes.

TEST YOURSELF ✔

Write 3 sentences about your partner's answers from 3B.

My partner has new shoes. He doesn't need a sweater. He wants new clothes.

1 Learn to buy clothes

A Look at the clothing ad. Complete the sentences.

SHOP & SAVE Labor Day Sale
Se... Uniforms All Colors - All Sizes

M L XL

$14.99 $16.99

Also On Sale Now!

$18.99

Men's sweatshirts 50% off S, M, L

$16.00 $8.00

1. The _____yellow_____ shirt is extra large (XL).
2. The _____ shirt is medium (M).
3. The _____ shirt is large (L).
4. The _____ shirt is small (S).

B Listen and read.

A: Excuse me. How much is this blouse?
B: It's on sale for $16.99. What size do you need?
A: I need a medium.
B: Here's a medium in red.
A: I'll take it.

Here's a medium.

C Listen again and repeat.

D Work with a partner. Practice the conversation. Use the clothing ad in 1A.

A: Excuse me. How much is this _____?
B: It's on sale for _____. What size do you need?
A: I need _____.
B: Here's a/an _____ in _____.
A: I'll take it.

✔ Select clothing based on sizes and prices

E Look at the pictures. Listen and write the sizes and the prices.

① Size: _____ Price: _____

② Size: _____ Price: _____

Size: _____ Price: _____

③ Size: _____ Price: _____

Size: _____ Price: _____

2 Practice your pronunciation

A Listen for the stress.

-teen	thir**teen**	four**teen**	fif**teen**	six**teen**	seven**teen**	eigh**teen**	nine**teen**
-ty	**thir**ty	**for**ty	**fif**ty	**six**ty	**seven**ty	**eigh**ty	**nine**ty

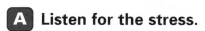

B Listen and repeat the numbers.

1. 40   3. 14   5. 90
2. 18   4. 13   6. 60

C Listen and circle the prices you hear. Compare answers with a partner.

1. $15.00   ($50.00)   3. $40.28 $14.28   5. $10.18 $10.80
2. $60.00 $16.00   4. $12.16 $12.60   6. $6.19 $6.90

3 Real-life math

Look at the receipt and read about Tanya. Then answer the question.

Tanya buys a sweater. The total is $18.48. She gives the salesperson a twenty-dollar bill. How much is her change? _____

```
****SHOP AND SAVE****

SWEATER          $16.99
TAX               $1.49

TOTAL            $18.48
```

TEST YOURSELF ✔

Work with a partner. Partner A: You're the customer. Tell your partner what you want to buy. Partner B: You're the salesperson. Help the customer. Then change roles.

1 Get ready to read

A Look at the pictures. Read the sentences.

Put your ATM card in the machine.

Withdraw your cash.

Take your cash, card, and receipt.

Count your money.

B Work with your classmates. Put the steps in order.

_____ Withdraw your cash.

_____ Take your cash, card, and receipt.

__1__ Put your ATM card in the machine.

_____ Count your money.

2 Read about ATMs

A Read the article.

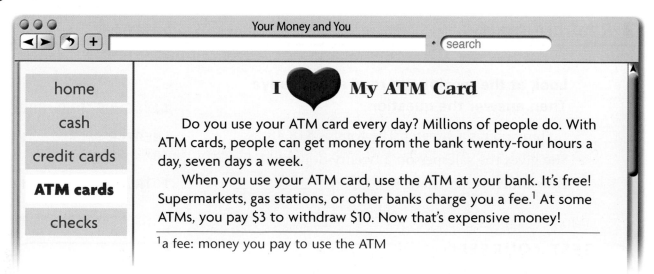

Your Money and You   search

home

cash

credit cards

ATM cards

checks

I ♥ My ATM Card

Do you use your ATM card every day? Millions of people do. With ATM cards, people can get money from the bank twenty-four hours a day, seven days a week.

When you use your ATM card, use the ATM at your bank. It's free! Supermarkets, gas stations, or other banks charge you a fee.[1] At some ATMs, you pay $3 to withdraw $10. Now that's expensive money!

[1] a fee: money you pay to use the ATM

Source: *www.fdic.gov*

STUDENT AUDIO

B Listen and read the article again.

☑ Interpret information about using an ATM; interpret a check

C Mark the sentences T (true) or F (false).

__T__ 1. Millions of people use ATM cards every day.

____ 2. People get money from ATMs seven days a week.

____ 3. Your bank's ATM charges you a fee.

____ 4. All ATMs charge fees.

D Complete the sentences. Use the words in the box.

free	fees	~~ATM card~~	millions

1. Use your _____ATM card_____ to get money from the bank.

2. Your bank's ATM is _____.

3. ATMs at other places often have _____.

4. _____ of people use ATM cards.

3 Read a check

A Kim Ling is writing a check. Look at the check. Answer the questions.

KIM LING   NO. **367**
218 Green St., Apt. 7
San Diego, CA 92299   DATE _April 19, 2007_

PAY TO THE
ORDER OF _Shop and Save_ $ _31.19_

Thirty-one dollars and nineteen cents ~~~~~~~~~~~~ DOLLARS

State Branch 22
Bank San Diego, CA 97311
                                                                        Kim Ling
3009421201 053252276

1. Who is writing the check? _____

2. How much money is she paying? _____

3. What store is she paying? _____

B Think about the question. Talk about the answers with your class.

What are some things people pay for with checks? Name 6 things.

BRING IT TO LIFE

Go shopping. Watch 5 people pay. Do people pay with cash, checks, or credit cards? Tell your classmates how people pay.

1 Grammar

A Circle *a* or *b*.

1. She has ____ new job at the bank.
   (a.) a   b. any

2. Do you have ____ brothers and sisters?
   a. a   b. any

3. We don't have ____ credit cards.
   a. a   b. any

4. I have ____ good friends.
   a. a   b. some

5. Does he have ____ new shirt?
   a. a   b. some

> **Grammar note**
>
> *a, some,* and *any*
>
> **Singular:** *a*
>
> A: Do you have a jacket?
> B: Yes, I have a jacket. *or*
> No, I don't have a jacket.
>
> **Plural:** *any/some*
>
> A: Do you have any socks?
> B: Yes, I have some socks. *or*
> No, I don't have any socks.

B Match the questions with the answers.

_c_ 1. Do you want a new jacket?   a. No, she doesn't.

____ 2. Is there an ATM near here?   b. Yes, there are.

____ 3. Do they need new books?   c. Yes, I do.

____ 4. Does she have a new car?   d. No, they don't.

____ 5. Does he like to shop?   e. Yes, he does.

____ 6. Are there any shirts on sale?   f. No, there isn't.

C Write the answers.

1. What do they want for dinner? (pizza) _They want pizza._

2. How much money does Pedro have? ($100) _____

3. What color suit does he want? (blue) _____

4. What do they need? (a new car) _____

5. When do you have lunch? (at 12:30 p.m.) _____

D Complete the story. Circle the correct words.

Today Emily ((is) / has) at the mall. She needs (some / any) new shoes. She
                       1   2

(want / wants) inexpensive brown shoes. There are some nice brown shoes (in / on) sale
   3   4

for $25. Emily (has / want) $40. She pays the (customer / salesperson). Her change
             5   6

(is / are) $15. She (have / likes) her new shoes.
  7   8

2 Group work

A Work with 2–3 classmates. Write 5 sentences about the picture on page 77. Talk about the sentences with your class.

A man is wearing a suit. A woman is buying a dress.

B Interview 3 classmates. Write their answers in your notebook.

ASK:

1. Do you have a favorite clothing store?
2. Do you want any new clothes?
3. Do you need any new work or school clothes?
4. Do you pay for clothes with cash, checks, or credit cards?

Classmate—Leticia
1. Yes, she does.
2. Yes, she does.
3. No, she doesn't.
4. cash

C Talk about the answers with your class.

PROBLEM SOLVING

A Listen and read about Joel. What is his problem?

Joel is at the bank. He wants $40. He puts his card in the ATM. He takes his card, his money, and his receipt. When he counts the money, he only has $20!

B Work with your classmates. Answer the question. (More than one answer may be possible.)

What can Joel do?
a. Call the police.
b. Put the card in the machine again.
c. Ask for help at the bank.
d. Other: _____

C Work with your classmates. Make a list of things Joel can say.

UNIT **8**

Eating Well

FOCUS ON
- food
- food shopping
- frequency expressions
- restaurant orders
- healthy eating habits

LESSON **1** Vocabulary

1 Learn food shopping words

A Look at the picture. Where are the people?

B Listen and look at the picture.

C Listen and repeat the words.

1. fruit   2. vegetables   3. basket   4. cart   5. checker   6. bagger

D Look at the picture. Complete the sentences.

1. The man in the white shirt is next to the _vegetables_, on the right.
2. The _____ is next to the vegetables, on the left.
3. The _____ has a yellow tie.
4. One woman has a red _____.
5. One man has a blue _____.
6. The _____ has a green blouse.

2 Talk about a supermarket

A Work with your classmates. Match the words with the picture.

___ apples	___ chicken	___ lettuce	___ potatoes
_1_ bananas	___ eggs	___ milk	___ soup
___ bread	___ grapes	___ onions	___ tomatoes

B Listen and check your answers. Then practice the words with a partner.

C Cross out (X) the item that does NOT belong in each group.

1. apples   bananas   le~~ttuce~~   grapes
2. checker   eggs   bagger   customer
3. bread   onions   potatoes   lettuce
4. chicken   bread   soup   cart

D Work with a partner. Talk about food shopping.

I buy milk, eggs, bread, and fruit every week.

I use a basket. I pay with a credit card.

How about you?

TEST YOURSELF ✔

Close your book. Write 5 food words and 5 supermarket words. Check your spelling in a dictionary.

1 Read about food shopping

  A **Look at the pictures. Listen.**

 B **Listen again. Read the sentences.**

1. The Garcias make a shopping list every Wednesday night.
2. They go to the supermarket every Thursday morning.
3. Mr. Garcia loves oranges. They get oranges every time they shop.
4. Every week, they buy chicken and fish.
5. Once or twice a month, they buy cookies or ice cream.
6. They always look for good prices.

C **Check your understanding. Mark the sentences T (true) or F (false).**

___T___ 1. The Garcias go to the market every Thursday.

_____ 2. They make a shopping list every Monday.

_____ 3. They buy chicken every week.

_____ 4. Mr. Garcia doesn't like oranges.

_____ 5. They buy cookies every day.

_____ 6. They always look for good prices.

90   ☑ Interpret food advertisements; write a shopping list

ssions

. Answer the questions below.

Tuesday	Wednesday	Thursday	Friday	Saturday
have dinner with Alex	cook dinner at home	cook dinner at home	order pizza 	have dinner with Alex

with Alex on Tuesdays and Saturdays? _____

pizza? _____

More frequency expressions

every day / week / month / year
once a day / week / month / year
twice a day / week / month / year
three times a day / week / month / year
never (0 times) *We never cook.*

th.

a year.

Use Lucy's schedule in 1A.

a week .

lex _____.

_____.

_____ cooks dinner on Friday.

ur own information. Read the sentences

dinner three times a week.

_____

) _____

e) _____

nple present

2 Write about food shopping

A Write about yourself. Complete

I go to the supermarket every _____

Every week, I buy _____

and _____ .

I love _____ .

I always look for _____

B Read your story to a partner.

3 Talk about food shopping

A Look at the supermarket ads. R

B Listen to the Garcias talk about
Check (✔) the items they are go

C Listen. Then practice the conve

A: Let's make vegetable soup.

B: We need some onions. Do we n

A: Yes, we do. Do we need any car

B: No, we have some.

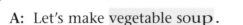
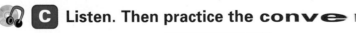
TEST YOURSELF ✔

Close your book. Write a shopping list.

ssions

. Answer the questions below.

Tuesday	Wednesday	Thursday	Friday	Saturday
have dinner with Alex	cook dinner at home	cook dinner at home	order pizza 	have dinner with Alex

with Alex on Tuesdays and Saturdays? _____

pizza? _____

More frequency expressions

every day / week / month / year
once a day / week / month / year
twice a day / week / month / year
three times a day / week / month / year
never (0 times) *We never cook.*

th.

a year.

Use Lucy's schedule in 1A.

a week   .

lex _____ .

_____ .

_____ cooks dinner on Friday.

our own information. Read the sentences

dinner three times a week.

_____

s) _____

ne) _____

imple present

2 Write about food shopping

A Write about yourself. Complete

I go to the supermarket every _____

Every week, I buy _____

and _____ .

I love _____ .

I always look for _____

B Read your story to a partner.

3 Talk about food shopping

A Look at the supermarket ads. R

  B Listen to the Garcias talk about _____
Check (✔) the items they are go

  C Listen. Then practice the conver

A: Let's make vegetable soup.

B: We need some onions. Do we ne

A: Yes, we do. Do we need any carr

B: No, we have some.

TEST YOURSELF ✓

Close your book. Write a shopping list. Te

1 Learn frequency expressions

A Look at Lucy's schedule. Answer the questions below.

Sunday	Monday	Tuesday	Wednesday	Thursday	Friday	Saturday
cook dinner at home	have dinner with Alex	cook dinner at home	cook dinner at home	order pizza	have dinner with Alex

1. Does Lucy have dinner with Alex on Tuesdays and Saturdays? _____
2. When does Lucy order pizza? _____

B Study the charts.

FREQUENCY EXPRESSI...

Frequency expressi...	
I cook	
Mary goes shopping	
We buy cookies	...th.
They order pizza	... a year.

More frequency expressions
every day / week / month / year
once a day / week / month / year
twice a day / week / month / year
three times a day / week / month / year
never (0 times) *We never cook.*

C Complete the sentence... Use Lucy's schedule in 1A.

1. Lucy orders pizza _once a week_.
   ...inner with Alex _____.
   ...dinner _____.
   _____ cooks dinner on Friday.

...ences with your own information. Read the sentences
...a partner.

(cook dinner) _I cook dinner three times a week._
(eat dinner at home) _____
(eat lunch with friends) _____
(have breakfast at home) _____

2 Write about food shopping

A **Write about yourself. Complete the sentences.**

I go to the supermarket every _____.

Every week, I buy _____, _____,

and _____.

I love _____.

I always look for _____.

Need help?

I buy...
   eggs.
   bread.
   milk.

B **Read your story to a partner.**

3 Talk about food shopping

A **Look at the supermarket ads. Read the items and the prices.**

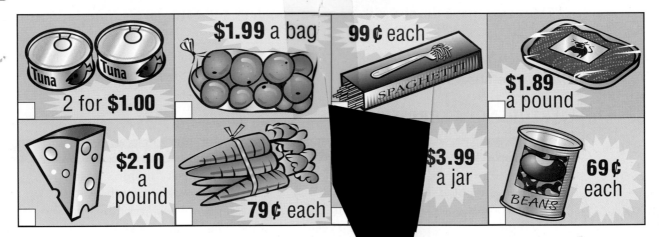

 STUDENT AUDIO **B** **Listen to the Garcias talk about the supermar___ ___ds. Check (✔) the items they are going to buy.**

STUDENT AUDIO **C** **Listen. Then practice the conversation with a partner.**

A: Let's make vegetable soup.

B: We need some onions. Do we need any potatoes?

A: Yes, we do. Do we need any carrots?

B: No, we have some.

salad

TEST YOURSELF ✔

Close your book. Write a shopping list. Tell a partner what's on your list.

2 Ask and answer questions with *How often*

A Study the chart. Ask and answer the questions.

Questions and answers with *How often*	
A: How often do you cook? **B:** I cook three times a day.	**A:** How often does he cook? **B:** He cooks twice a week.
A: How often do you cook? **B:** We cook every evening.	**A:** How often does she cook? **B:** She never cooks.

B Complete the questions. Then match the questions with the answers. Use the schedule from 1A.

_____ 1. How _____ does Lucy order pizza?   a. twice a week

_____ 2. How often do Lucy and Alex _____ dinner?   b. never

_____ 3. How often _____ Lucy cook on Fridays?   c. once a week

3 Practice questions about routines

A Read the questions. Write your answers in the chart.

Questions	My answers	My partner's answers
1. How often do you eat dinner with friends?		
2. How often do you order pizza?		
3. How often do you eat dinner at a restaurant?		
4. How often do you cook dinner at home?		

B Interview a partner. Write your partner's answers in the chart.

C Talk about the answers in the chart with your class.

I eat dinner with friends once a week. Mia eats dinner with friends three times a week.

TEST YOURSELF ✔

Write 4 sentences about your partner's answers from 3B.

Martin cooks dinner at home three times a week. He orders pizza once a week.

1 Learn to order food

A Look at the menu. Write the prices.

Pappa's Pizza Place

Menu

Pizza

Small pizza $6.50

Medium pizza $8.50

Large pizza $12.00

Toppings $1.00 each

pepperoni   onions

mushrooms   peppers

Drinks

Soda   Iced Tea

Small $1.50   Medium $1.75   Large $2.00

1. A large pepperoni pizza is ___$13.00___ .

2. A medium mushroom pizza is _____.

3. A small pizza with peppers and onions is _____.

4. A medium pepperoni and mushroom pizza is _____.

B Listen and read.

A: Are you ready to order?

B: Yes, I am—a medium pizza with onions, please.

A: Do you want anything to drink?

B: Yes, I do. I'd like a small iced tea.

A: OK, that's one medium pizza with onions and a small iced tea.

B: That's right.

C Listen again and repeat.

D Work with a partner. Practice the conversation. Use the menu in 1A.

A: Are you ready to order?

B: Yes, I am—a _____ pizza with _____, please.

A: Do you want anything to drink?

B: Yes, I do. I'd like _____.

A: OK, that's one _____ pizza with _____ and _____.

B: That's right.

E **Listen and complete the orders.**

1

GUEST CHECK				
Date	Table	Guests	Server	128354

_____large pizzas
with onions

1_____ pizza with
pepperoni

_____ _____sodas

Total

Thank you! Please come again.

2

Guest Check				
Date	Table	Guests	Server	7742

_____ _____

pizza with peppers

_____ _____

iced teas

_____ _____

_____

Total

Thank you! Please come again.

3

GUEST CHECK				
Date	Table	Guests	Server	410121

_____ _____

pizzas with _____
and _____

_____small _____

_____ _____

_____

Total

Thank you! Please come again.

2 Practice your pronunciation

  A **Listen to the question and answer.**

A: Are you ready to order?

B: Yes, I am.

  B **Listen and circle *question* or *answer*.**

1. question   answer
2.

3. question   answer
4. question   answer

[blacked out] the answers. Then practice with a partner.

_____der?   a. I want a small soda.

_____toppings?   b. Yes, I am.

Do you want anything to drink?   c. Yes, I do. Mushrooms, please.

3 Real-life math

Write the prices and the totals for the orders in 1E.
Use the menu in 1A.

TEST YOURSELF ✔

Work with a partner. Look at the menu on page 94. Partner A: Order a pizza
and a drink. Partner B: Repeat the order. Then change roles.

1 Get ready to read

A **Read the definitions.**

healthy: something that is good for your body

unhealthy: something that is not good for your body

B **Work with your classmates. Complete the chart with healthy food.**

Healthy food	
apples	

C **Circle the food in the chart that you eat every week.**

2 Read about healthy food

A **Read the article.**

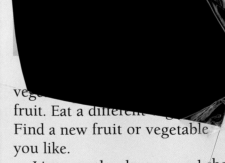

Doctors say, "Eat fruit and vegetables every day!"

Doctors and nutritionists[1] say, "Fruit and vegetables are good for you! Eat a lot of them every day." Some people don't listen. They say, "Fruit is expensive," or, "I don't like vegetables."

Do you think fruit and vegetables are expensive? Look at supermarket ads. Fruit and vegetables are on sale every week.

ve⟨...⟩ fruit. Eat a different ⟨...⟩ Find a new fruit or vegetable ⟨...⟩ you like.

Listen to the doctors and the nutritionists. Don't eat a lot of unhealthy food. Eat fruit and vegetables every day and be healthy!

[1]nutritionist: a person who teaches, talks, and writes about healthy food

Source: *www.cdc.gov*

STUDENT AUDIO

B **Listen and read the article again.**

☑ Identify healthy eating habits; interpret nutrition labels

C Mark the sentences T (true) or F (false).

___T___ 1. Doctors say, "Eat fruit every day."

_____ 2. Fruit and vegetables are unhealthy.

_____ 3. Fruit and vegetables are never on sale.

_____ 4. Nutritionists say, "Fruit is expensive."

D Complete the sentences. Use the words in the box.

| fruit | ~~healthy~~ | sale | nutritionists | vegetables |

1. Eat ___healthy___ food.
2. Doctors and _____ say, "Eat a lot of fruit and vegetables."
3. _____ and _____ are good for you.
4. Look for fruit and vegetables on _____ every week.

3 Read food labels

A Work with your classmates. Write the names of the soups.

(1)
Ingredients
water,
tomatoes,
salt

(2)
Ingredients
water,
chicken,
onions,
carrots

Salt-free!

(3)
Ingredients
water,
onions,
carrots,
mushrooms,
peppers,
tomatoes,
salt

___tomato soup___   _____   _____

B Look at the food labels. Complete the sentences.

1. The ___chicken___ soup has no salt.
2. The _____ soup has a lot of vegetables.
3. The _____ soup has three ingredients.

C Think about the questions. Talk about the answers with your class.

1. Do you think it's important to read food labels? Why or why not?
2. How often do you read the labels on food you buy?

BRING IT TO LIFE

Bring a food label to class. Talk about the ingredients with your classmates.

1 Grammar

A Circle the correct words.

1. I study (**every** / twice) day.
2. She (always / once) buys apples.
3. They (usually / three times) ride the bus.
4. Pat washes the windows (twice / one) a year.
5. They shop (always / once) a week.
6. Sharon pays the bills (never / three times) a month.

> **Grammar note**
>
> **Adverbs of frequency**
>
> always   100%
> usually
> sometimes
> never   0%
>
> I always eat breakfast.
> I usually eat eggs for breakfast.
> I sometimes eat breakfast at home.
> I never eat pizza for breakfast.

B Match the sentences with the frequency expressions.

__e__ 1. Frank watches a movie every Friday.

____ 2. Beth cleans the garage in May and October.

____ 3. She goes to the bank on the 1st and 15th of the month.

____ 4. I feed the cat in the morning, at noon, and at night.

____ 5. Gary and Elaine don't drink soda.

____ 6. She brushes her teeth in the morning and at night.

a. twice a day

b. twice a month

c. twice a year

d. three times a day

e. once a week

f. never

C Unscramble the sentences.

1. never / Lucy / Sunday / eats / on / dinner _Lucy never eats dinner on Sunday._
2. eats / once / Mrs. Mack / a week / ice cream _____
3. twice / Ben / does / homework / a week / usually _____
4. Sherman / a week / three / exercises / times _____
5. always / Alicia / English / speaks / at home _____

D Write the answers.

1. How often do you go shopping? _I go shopping twice a week._
2. How often do you buy ice cream? _____
3. How often do you cook dinner for friends? _____
4. How often do you clean the kitchen? _____

2 Group work

A Work with 2–3 classmates. Look at the picture on page 89.
Write 5 *How often?* questions about the food in the picture.
Talk about the questions with your class.

How often do you buy bread? How often do you buy oranges?

B Interview 3 classmates. Write their answers in your notebook.

ASK:

1. How often do you eat vegetables
   with your dinner?
2. How often do you order pizza?
3. How often do you cook dinner?

Classmate—Ching Fu
1. every day
2. once or twice
   a month
3. never

C Talk about the answers with your class.

PROBLEM SOLVING

A Listen and read about the Ruzika family. What is
the problem?

Sam and Lia Ruzika have two daughters. Every night at
dinner the children say, "We don't like vegetables." Lia and
Sam think, "Our girls need vegetables." Lia cooks different
vegetables every night. She cooks broccoli, mushrooms,
potatoes, and carrots. The girls never eat them. They say
the same thing, "We don't like vegetables."

B Work with your classmates. Answer the question.
(More than one answer is possible.)

What can Lia and Sam do?
 a. Order pizza with vegetables on it.
 b. Give the girls a lot of fruit.
 c. Tell the girls that vegetables are healthy.
 d. Other: _____

C Work with your classmates. Make a list of things Lia and Sam can say.

Your Health

FOCUS ON
- parts of the body/illness and injuries
- medical instructions and advice
- the verb phrase *have to*
- making medical appointments
- preventive care and medicine

LESSON **1**   Vocabulary

1 Learn about parts of the body

A Look at the pictures. Is Mr. Patel healthy?

B Listen and look at the pictures.

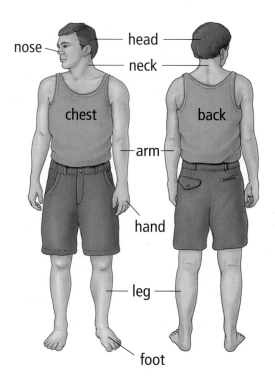

Ms. Lee   Mr. Diaz   Ms. Singh

Mr. Patel   Mr. Gold   Ms. Vega

C Listen and repeat the words.

1. head   3. neck   5. chest   7. hand   9. leg
2. nose   4. back   6. arm   8. foot*

*one foot / two feet

D Look at the pictures. Complete the sentences.

1. Ms. Lee's ___head___ hurts.
2. Mr. Diaz's _____ hurts.
3. Mr. Patel's _____ hurts.
4. Ms. Singh's _____ and _____ hurt.
5. Mr. Gold's _____ and _____ hurt.
6. Ms. Vega's _____ and _____ hurt.

2 Talk about a doctor's office

A Work with your classmates. Match the words with the picture.

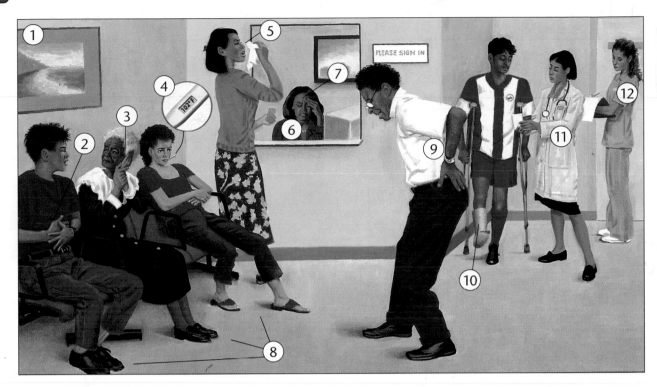

9	backache	11	doctor	4	fever	8	patients
10	broken leg	1	doctor's office	7	headache	6	receptionist
5	cold	3	earache	12	nurse	2	stomachache

B Listen and check your answers. Then practice the words with a partner.

C Cross out (X) the item that does NOT belong in each group.

1. nurse   stoma~~ch~~ache   receptionist   doctor
2. patients   earache   stomachache   headache
3. eyes   mouth   cold   nose
4. arms   legs   nose   hands

D Work with a partner. Ask and answer questions. Use the picture in 2A.

A: What's the matter with the man in the white shirt?

B: He has a backache. What's the matter with the receptionist?

A: Her head hurts. She has a headache.

TEST YOURSELF ✔

Close your book. Write 6 body words and 4 illness and injury words. Check your spelling in a dictionary.

1 Read about a doctor's appointment

  A **Look at the pictures. Listen.**

 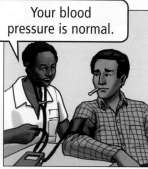

Your blood pressure is normal.

 B **Listen again. Read the sentences.**

1. Miguel is sick today. He's at the doctor's office. He has a sore throat.
2. He gives his insurance card to the receptionist.
3. The nurse takes his temperature and his blood pressure.
4. Miguel opens his mouth. The doctor examines him and writes a prescription.
5. Miguel has to take his prescription medicine twice a day.
6. Miguel has to stay home and rest. He wants to get well.

get well

C **Check your understanding. Circle the correct words.**

1. Miguel has a sore ((throat) / mouth).
2. Miguel needs his insurance (car / (card)).
3. The nurse takes his ((temperature) / medicine).
4. The doctor examines ((him) / a prescription).
5. Miguel has to take prescription medicine (once / (twice)) a day.
6. Miguel has to stay home and ((rest) / chest).

2 Write about yourself

A **Write your story. Complete the sentences.**

Sometimes I have a / an _____, and I go to the
doctor. _____ takes my temperature and blood
pressure. _____ examines me and gives me a
prescription. I _____ to get well.

B **Read your story to a partner.**

Need help?

Ways to get well
stay home
rest
take medicine

3 Talk about ways to get well and to stay healthy

A Look at the pictures. Read the ways to get well and to stay healthy.

Ⓐ Take medicine.

Ⓑ Rest.

Ⓒ Change your diet.

Ⓓ Exercise.

Ⓔ Drink fluids.

Ⓕ Quit smoking.

STUDENT
AUDIO

B Listen to the conversations. Match the doctor's advice in 3A with the correct patients.

1. Mr. Jones ___c___
2. Mrs. Lynn _____
3. Mr. Martinez _____
4. Ms. Mendoza _____
5. Mr. White _____
6. Mr. Wang _____

STUDENT
AUDIO

C Listen and repeat.

A: What do you do for a sore throat?
B: I take medicine. What do you do?
A: I drink tea.

D Work with a partner. Practice the conversation. Use your own ideas.

TEST YOURSELF ✔

Close your book. Tell a partner 3 ways to get well. Change roles. Listen and write your partner's ideas.

1 Learn *have to*

A Look at the pictures. Read the sentences. Where does Jeff have to go?

Maria has to leave class early. She has to pick up her son.

Jeff has to leave work early. He has to go to the dentist.

Kim and Rosa have to leave the party early. They have to study.

B Study the chart. Complete the sentences below.

HAVE TO

Statements						
I You	have to	go to the dentist.		We You	have to	go to the dentist.
He She	has to			They		

1. He _____ go to the dentist.   2. They _____ go to the dentist.

C Look at the pictures. Circle the correct words.

1. Maria (⟨has⟩ / has to) a son.
2. Jeff (⟨has to⟩ / have to) go to the dentist.
3. He (has to / has) a toothache.
4. Kim and Rosa (has to / have to) study.
5. They (have / have to) a test tomorrow.
6. They (have / have to) leave early.

D Work with a partner. Talk about things you have to do this week.

A: *I have to study. How about you?*

B: *I have to go to the bank.*

2 Ask and answer information questions with *have to*

A Study the chart. Ask and answer the questions.

Information questions and answers with *have to*	
A: Why do you have to leave early? **B:** I have to pick up my children.	**A:** Why does he have to leave early? **B:** He has to go to the doctor.
A: Why do they have to leave early? **B:** They have to study.	**A:** Why does she have to leave early? **B:** She has to go to the dentist.

B Match the questions with the answers.

_d_ 1. Why do you have to leave early?

____ 2. Why does Jeff have to go to the dentist?

____ 3. Why does Maria have to talk to the teacher?

____ 4. Why do the girls have to go to the library?

____ 5. Why does Miguel have to see the doctor?

a. She has to leave early.

b. He has a sore throat.

c. They have to study.

d. I have to pick up my son.

e. He has a toothache.

3 Practice *have to*

A Complete the questions with the words in the box.
Then write your answers.

~~Why~~ What When Where

1. __Why__ do you have to come to class every day? __I have to practice English.__

2. _____ do you have to do after class today? _____

3. _____ do you have to go after class? _____

4. _____ do you have to get up tomorrow? _____

B Ask and answer the questions in 3A with a partner. Then write 4 sentences about your partner's answers.

Teresa has to practice English.

C Talk about the sentences with your class.

Teresa has to practice English. She has to make lunch after class.

TEST YOURSELF ✔

Close your book. Write 5 things you have to do this week. Use complete sentences.

1 Learn to make an appointment

A Read the appointment card. Answer the questions.

> Dear *Vera* ,
>
> ### YOU HAVE AN APPOINTMENT
>
> With: *Dr. Brown*
>
> On: *Monday, May 12th*
>
> At: *3:00* a.m. (p.m)
>
> See you then!
>
> (M)   T   W   TH   F

1. Who has an appointment with Dr. Brown? _____ Vera _____
2. What day is the appointment? _____
3. What's the date of the appointment? _____
4. What time is the appointment? _____

B Listen and read.

A: Hello, doctor's office.
B: Hello. This is Carl Lee. I have a terrible cold. *bachache.*
   I have to see the doctor.
A: Let's see. I have an opening on Wednesday at 2:00. *thursday* *ada*
   Is that OK?
B: Yes, it is. Thanks. *iris*
A: OK. See you on Wednesday, May 12th at 2:00. *Febrery* *3:00pm*
   28

C Listen again and repeat.

D Work with a partner. Practice the conversation. Use your own
information.

A: I have a terrible _____. I have to see the doctor.
B: Let's see. I have an opening on _*thursday*_, *28 at 2:00pm*
   at _____. Is that OK? *Febrery*
A: Yes, it is. Thanks.
B: OK. See you on _*thursday*_ at _____.

STUDENT AUDIO **E** Listen and complete the appointment cards.

1

Dear __Tom__,

YOU HAVE AN APPOINTMENT

With: __Dr. Wu__

On: _____

At: _____ a.m. p.m

M   T   W   TH   F

2

Dear _____,

YOU HAVE AN APPOINTMENT

With: _____

On: __oct 24__

At: __10:30__ a.m. (p.m)

M   T   W   TH   F

2 Learn prepositions *on* and *at*

A Complete the sentences with *on* or *at*.

1. I have to leave _____at_____ 5:00.
2. Sue has an appointment _____on_____ Tuesday.
3. We want to go to the party _____at_____ 7.00.
4. I have to see the doctor _____on_____ June 17th.

> ### Grammar note
>
> **on or at?**
>
> Use *on* for days and dates.
>   on Monday
>   on November 11th
>
> Use *at* for times.
>   at 10:30
>   at noon

B Write your answers.

1. When do you have to come to class? _____
2. When do you have to go to work? _____
3. When do you have to get up tomorrow? _____

3 Practice your pronunciation

STUDENT AUDIO **A** Listen to the sentences.

1. I **have to** see the doctor.
    I **have a** cold.

2. She **has to** go at 2:30.
    She **has a** new job.

B Listen again and repeat.

STUDENT AUDIO **C** Listen and circle the words you hear.

1. (have to)   have   3. has to   has
2. have to   has to   4. have   has

TEST YOURSELF ✔

Work with a partner. Make an appointment to see a doctor. Partner A:
You're the patient. Partner B: You're the receptionist. Then change roles.

LESSON 5 Real-life reading

1 Get ready to read

A Look at the picture. Read the definitions.

checkup: a medical examination to check your health when you are not sick

over-the-counter medicine: medicine you don't need a prescription to buy

B Work with your classmates. How often do you do these things?

1. exercise   2. eat healthy food   3. get a checkup

2 Read about good health

A Read the article.

Feeling Fine
It's not always easy to be healthy. Here are some ways to be healthy and feel good.

Exercise
Doctors say it's important to exercise for thirty minutes a day, three days a week.

Eat healthy food
Don't forget to eat fruit and vegetables. They're good for you, and they taste good.

Have regular checkups
See your doctor for a checkup once a year. Always follow your doctor's health instructions.

If you feel sick, you can take over-the-counter medicine. Sometimes over-the-counter medicine helps people feel better. It's important to read and follow the directions exactly.[1] Over-the-counter medicines don't always stop the problem. Then, you have to go to the doctor.

[1]exactly = with no mistakes

  B Listen and read the article again.

C **Circle the correct words.**

1. It's important to have a checkup every (month /(year)).
2. Eat ((fruit and vegetables)/ over-the-counter medicine) every day.
3. It's important to exercise ((three)/ thirty) days a week.
4. Always (feel /(follow)) the directions with over-the-counter medicine.

D **Complete the sentences. Use the words in the box.**

checkup	~~feel~~	exactly	healthy

1. Over-the-counter medicine can help you _____feel_____ better.
2. It's a good idea to go to the doctor for a _____checkup_____ every year.
3. Follow all the directions _____exeactly_____ with over-the-counter medicine.
4. Exercise can help you be _____healthy_____ and feel good.

3 Read directions and warnings on medicine labels

A **Look at the medicine labels. Match the sentences with the labels.**

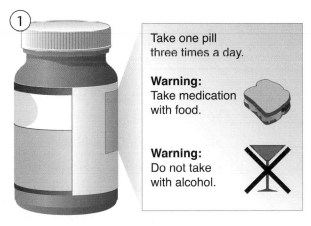

Take one pill three times a day.

Warning:
Take medication with food.

Warning:
Do not take with alcohol.

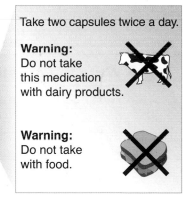

Take two capsules twice a day.

Warning:
Do not take this medication with dairy products.

Warning:
Do not take with food.

1. Do not take this with milk. _2_
2. Take this medicine with food. _1_
3. Do not take this with alcohol. _1_
4. Take this medicine twice a day. _2_
5. Do not take this with food. _2_
6. Take this medicine three times a day. _1_

B **Think about the question. Talk about the answer with your class.**

What other warnings are on medicine labels? Name or draw 2 other warnings you know.

BRING IT TO LIFE

Go to a pharmacy. Look at a medicine label. Write the name of the medicine. Write or draw the directions and warnings in your notebook.

1 Grammar

A Circle the correct words.

1. The (**woman** / women) has a cold.
2. This (**child** / children) has to see the dentist.
3. Those (person / **people**) have to ride the bus.
4. His (teeth / **tooth**) hurts.
5. My (foot / **feet**) hurt.
6. The (man / men) have to talk to the nurse.
      mean

> **Grammar note**
>
> **Irregular plural nouns**
>
> | Singular | Plural |
> |----------|--------|
> | foot 1 | feet 2 |
> | tooth | teeth |
> | man | men |
> | woman | women |
> | child | children |
> | person | people |

B Match the questions with the answers.

__e__ 1. What's the matter with Maria?   a. He has to see the doctor.

__d__ 2. When does she have to leave?   b. No, he doesn't.

____ 3. Why does Carl have to leave early?   c. We leave early once a week.

____ 4. Does he leave early every day?   d. She has to leave at 2:00.

____ 5. How often do you leave early?   e. She has a backache.

C Write the questions.

1. _Does Rosa have to leave early?_____ Yes, she has to leave early.
2. _____ She has a stomachache.
3. _____ She has to leave at 10:30.
4. _____ She has to go to the doctor.
5. _____ No, she doesn't always leave early.

D Complete the story. Use the words in the box.

| ~~is~~   have   at   isn't   has   on   receptionist   has to   wants |

Today ____is____ Monday. Mr. Larson _____ an earache.
       1   2

He _____ see the doctor. He talks to the _____.
    3   4

The doctor doesn't _____ an opening today. There's an
                       5

opening _____ Tuesday _____ 10:00.
       6   7

Mr. Larson _____ happy. He _____ to see the doctor today.
               8   9

2 Group work

A Work with 2–3 classmates. Write 5 sentences about the picture on page 101. Talk about the sentences with your class.

A woman is sitting in the chair. She has an earache.

B Interview 3 classmates. Write their answers in your notebook.

ASK:

1. What do you have to do this afternoon?
2. How often do you have to clean the house?
3. Do you have to work this weekend?

Classmate–Rafik

1. go to the bank
2. once a week
3. yes

C Talk about the answers with your class.

PROBLEM SOLVING

A Listen and read about David. What is his problem?

David teaches English in the evening. He likes his job and his students very much. Every day he tells his students, "You have to come to school every day. Don't stay home! Come and learn English every day." David has a problem today. He has a terrible headache and a stomachache, too. He doesn't want to go home, but he feels terrible.

B Work with your classmates. Answer the question. (More than one answer is possible.)

What can David do?
   a. Call the doctor.
   b. Go home now.
   c. Stay at school now, but stay home tomorrow.
   d. Other: _____

C Work with your classmates. What can David tell his students?

UNIT 10

Getting the Job

FOCUS ON
- jobs and job skills
- looking for a job
- the simple past of *be*
- job interviews
- good employee skills

LESSON 1 Vocabulary

1 Learn names of jobs

A Look at the pictures. Point to the person cleaning a school.

STUDENT AUDIO

B Listen and look at the pictures.

STUDENT AUDIO

C Listen and repeat the words.

1. pharmacist 3. mechanic 5. server
2. homemaker 4. janitor 6. childcare worker

D Look at the pictures. Complete the sentences.

1. A _____mechanic_____ works in a garage.
2. A _____ works at home.
3. A _____ works in a childcare center.
4. A _____ works at a school.
5. A _____ works in a pharmacy.
6. A _____ works in a restaurant.

2 Talk about jobs and skills

A Work with your classmates. Match the words with the picture.

____ bus person   <u>1</u> delivery person   ____ manager   ____ plumber

____ cook   ____ gardener   <u>7</u> painter   ____ server

B Listen and check your answers. Then practice the words with a partner.

C Complete the sentences.

1. A ____plumber____ fixes sinks.
2. A _____ cleans tables.
3. A _____ works in gardens.
4. A _____ cooks food.

5. A _____ delivers packages.
6. A _____ manages a business.
7. A _____ serves food.
8. A _____ paints buildings.

D Work with a partner. Ask and answer questions about jobs. Use the picture in 2A.

A: Who is he?

B: He's a cook.

A: What's he doing?

B: He's cooking.

TEST YOURSELF ✔

Close your book. Write 5 jobs and 5 job skills. Check your spelling in a dictionary.

1 Read about getting a job

  A **Look at the pictures. Listen.**

  B **Listen again. Read the sentences.**

1. Sergei was a pharmacist in Russia. Now he lives in New York.
2. He's looking for a job.
3. He looks at the help-wanted ads in the newspaper.
4. He sees a sign in a pet store window and applies for the job.
5. He has an interview and gets the job.
6. Sergei is happy. He loves his new job.

C **Check your understanding. Mark the sentences T (true) or F (false).**

_F_ 1. Sergei lives in Russia now.   ____ 4. He sees a sign on the Internet.

____ 2. He is a pharmacist in New York.   ____ 5. He gets a job.

____ 3. He looks in the newspaper for a job. ____ 6. He loves his job.

2 Write about looking for a job

A **Write about how to look for a job. Complete the sentences.**

Are you looking for a job?

You can look _____ or look

_____ to find a job.

Then, you _____ and

have an _____. Good luck!

> **Need help?**
>
> **You can look...**
>
> in the newspaper.
> in store windows.
> on the Internet.

B **Read your sentences to a partner.**

3 Read help-wanted ads

A Look at the help-wanted ads. Read about the jobs.

1.
HELP WANTED
Driver
Evenings, part-time
(18 hours a week)
Call Tom.
555-2298

2.
Mechanic Needed
FT (40 hours a week)
See Bill.
Southside Auto Repair
9245 Clark Avenue

3.
Manager Needed
Full-time
Apply at Pizza King.
227 Main Street

4.
HELP WANTED
Cleaning staff
PT (25 hours a week),
late nights
Call Carla for an application.
555 8841

B Look at the help-wanted ads again. Read the sentences.
Check (✔) the correct boxes.

	Job #1	Job #2	Job #3	Job #4
1. This job is part-time (PT).	✔			✔
2. This job is full-time (FT).				
3. This job is on Main Street.				
4. This job is in the evenings.				
5. You have to talk to Bill for this job.				
6. You have to talk to Carla for this job.				

C Work with a partner. Ask and answer questions
about the help-wanted ads in 3A.

1. What's the job?
2. Is it part-time or full-time?
3. How many hours is the job?
4. Who can I talk to about the job?

TEST YOURSELF ✔

Close your book. Write a help-wanted ad for a job you want. Share your ad
with a partner.

1 Learn the simple past with *be*

A Look at the pictures. Was Rico a student or a gardener in 1992?

farmer 1980–1991   student 1991–1993   gardener 1994–2002   business owner 2002–present

B Study the charts. Complete the sentences below.

THE SIMPLE PAST WITH *BE*

Statements						
I	was		We			
You	were	a gardener.	You	were	gardeners.	
He She	was		They			

1. He __was__ a gardener.   2. They __were__ gardeners.

Negative statements						
I	was not		We			
You	were not	a gardener.	You	were not	gardeners.	
He She	was not		They			

Contractions
was not = wasn't I wasn't a gardener. were not = weren't They weren't gardeners.

3. He __was not__ a gardener.   4. We __weren't__ gardeners.

C Complete the sentences. Use the information in 1A.

1. Rico _____was_____ a farmer in 1980.
2. Rico and his brothers _____they_____ gardeners in 1994.
3. They __were not__ gardeners in 1981.
4. Rico __was not__ a student in 2001.

☑ Use the simple past of *be* to describe work experience

2 Ask and answer *Yes/No* questions

A Study the chart. Ask and answer the questions.

Yes/No questions and answers	
A: Were you a doctor ten years ago? **B:** Yes, I was. *or* No, I wasn't.	**A:** Were you at home last night? **B:** Yes, we were. *or* No, we weren't.
A: Was he a student five months ago? **B:** Yes, he was. *or* No, he wasn't.	**A:** Were they at school last week? **B:** Yes, they were. *or* No, they weren't.

B Match the questions with the answers.

_c_ 1. Were they at home yesterday?　　　　a. Yes, he was.

_d_ 2. Was she a student in Brazil?　　　　b. No, I wasn't.

_b_ 3. Were you a student six years ago?　　c. No, they weren't.

_a_ 4. Was he at school last week?　　　　d. Yes, she was.

C Complete the questions. Then write the answers.

1. __Was__ Rico a farmer 25 years ago? __Yes, he was.__
2. __was__ Rico a student last year? __No, he wosn't__
3. __Were__ you a student in 2004? __No, I wosn't__
4. __were__ you at school yesterday? __NO, I wash't__

3 Practice *Yes/No* questions

A Complete the questions with a job. Write your answers.

1. In your home country, were you (a) / an ___gardener___ ? _____
2. In your home country, were you a / an ___former___ ? _____
3. In your home country, were you a / an _____ ? _____

B Ask and answer the questions in 3A with a partner. Then write sentences about your partner's answers.

Juan was a gardener in Guatemala.

TEST YOURSELF ✔

Close your book. Write 2 to 4 sentences about your work experience.

I was a homemaker from 1990 to 1998. I was a server from 1998 to 2002.

1 Learn about a job interview

A Read Isabel Monte's job application. Match the questions with the answers.

Applicant name: *Isabel Monte*	Position: *Office Assistant*
Experience:	Skills: *use a computer, make copies,*
Receptionist 2005-present Los Angeles	*answer phones, speak English and Spanish*
Office Manager 1995-2005 Guatemala City	Education: *English classes,*
Office Assistant 1988-1995 Guatemala City	*computer classes, business classes*

_d_ 1. When was Isabel an office manager?   a. Guatemala City

_c_ 2. Does she have office skills?   b. office assistant

_a_ 3. Where was she in 1998?   c. yes

_b_ 4. What job does she want?   d. from 1995 to 2005

B Listen and read.

A: Tell me about yourself, Mr. Tran.

B: I'm from Vietnam. I lived there for thirty years.

A: Do you have work experience?

B: Yes, I do. I was a restaurant manager for two years.
I can cook, serve food, and wash dishes, too.

A: Can you work weekends?

B: Yes, I can.

A: That's great. You're hired!

C Listen again and repeat.

D Work with a partner. Practice the conversation. Use
your own information.

A: Tell me about yourself, <u>Mr. Jose</u>.

B: I'm from <u>Mexico city</u>. I lived there
for <u>fifteen</u> years.

A: Do you have work experience?

B: Yes, I do. I was a _____ for _____ years.
I can _____ and _____.

A: That's great. You're hired!

> **Need help?**
>
> A: Do you have work experience?
> B: Yes, I do. *or*
>   No, I don't, but I can learn quickly.

E Listen and match the people with the job skills.

_b_ 1. Gladys   a. He can fix sinks and toilets.

_c_ 2. Ken   b. She can help patients.

_a_ 3. Franco   c. He can fill prescriptions.

_d_ 4. Molly   d. She can cook, clean, pay bills, and take care of children.

2 Learn questions with *can*

A Study the chart. Complete the sentences below.

Questions with *can*		
Can	you he she they	fix cars?

Answers					
Yes,	I he she they	can.	No,	I he she they	can't.

1. **A:** Can he ___Fix___ cars?
   B: Yes, he ___can___.

2. **A:** ___Yes___ he fix sinks?
   B: No, he ___can't___.

B Work with a partner. Ask and answer questions with *can*.

A: Can you fix cars?   A: Can you manage a restaurant?

B: Yes, I can.   B: No, I can't.

3 Practice your pronunciation

A Listen and repeat.

Can	Can't
I can ride a bicycle.	I can't drive a bus.
Jose can speak English.	He can't speak Chinese.

B Listen for *can* or *can't*. Circle *a* or *b*.

1. a. can   (b.) can't   3. (a.) can   b. can't   5. a. can   (b.) can't

2. a. (can)   b. can't   4. a. can   (b.) can't   6. (a.) can   b. can't

TEST YOURSELF ✔

Work with a partner. Tell a partner about 3 job skills you have. Then change roles.

I can fix sinks, I can speak English and Chinese, and I can drive a truck.

1 Get ready to read

A **Read the definitions.**

employee: worker

boss: the person you work for; your supervisor or manager

co-workers: people who work with you; other employees

B **Work with your classmates. Which questions can you ask your boss? Which questions can you ask your co-workers?**

1. Can I leave early today?
2. How do I use the photocopier?
3. Do you like your job here?
4. Where's the lunchroom?

2 Read about great employees

A **Read the quiz. Then answer the questions.**

Are You Good or Are You Great?

Are you a good employee, or a great employee? Check (✔) *yes* or *no* for each sentence. Then count the number of *yes* answers you have. Read what your answers say about you.

1 I always read memos[1] and employee information from my boss.

Yes _____ No _____

2 I ask my co-workers for help or advice.

Yes _____ No _____

3 I come to work on time or a little early every day.

Yes _____ No _____

4 I call my boss on days I can't come to work.

Yes _____ No _____

5 I complete my time card on time.

Yes _____ No _____

What your answers say about you:
5 yes answers: You are an excellent employee!
3–4 yes answers: You are working hard. You're a good employee!
1–2 yes answers: Need help? Ask a co-worker. You can learn something new every day.

[1]memo: a note from a boss to the employee(s)

 B **Listen and read the quiz again.**

STUDENT AUDIO

☑ Identify appropriate workplace behavior; interpret a time card

C Complete the sentences. Circle *a* or *b*.

1. Ask your co-workers for ____.

   (a.) help   b. memos

2. A memo is usually from the ____.

   a. employees   b. boss

3. Call your ____ on days you can't work.

   a. co-worker   b. boss

4. Come to work ____.

   a. on time   b. sometimes

3 Read a time card

A Look at the time card. Complete the sentences.

Quick Stop Car Wash   **Employee Time Card**

Name: **White, Joey**   Employee number: **0521**   Rate: **$12.50**   Pay Period: **June 1–June 7**

Day	Time in	Time out	Hours
Monday	8:00 a.m.	2:00 p.m.	6
Wednesday	8:00 a.m.	2:00 p.m.	6
Friday	8:00 a.m.	2:00 p.m.	6
Total hours:			18

1. A pay period at Quick Stop Car Wash is _____ days.

2. Joey was at work on _____, _____ and _____.

3. Joey was at work from _____ to _____ on Monday.

B Think about the questions. Talk about the answers with your class.

1. Is the rate of pay at Quick Stop Car Wash good?
2. Is Joey's work schedule a good work schedule for you? Why or why not?

4 Real-life math

Look at Joey's time card again. Answer the questions.

Joey works the same schedule every week.

1. How much money does he make every pay period? _____

2. How much money does he make in a year? _____

BRING IT TO LIFE

Find magazine pictures of employees and bosses at work. Bring the pictures to class. Talk about the pictures with your classmates.

1 Grammar

A **Complete the sentences with *can* or *can't*.**

1. I can speak English,
   and Henry _____can_____, too.

2. My son can cook,
   but my daughter _____.

3. I can take care of children,
   and Jackie _____, too.

4. I can fix sinks, and I _____ fix bathtubs, too.

5. David _____ speak English, but he can't speak Spanish.

6. Bill can help patients, but he _____ manage a restaurant.

> **Grammar note**
>
> ***and/too***
> I can cook. Mary can cook.
> I can cook, **and** Mary can, too.
> ***but***
> I can cook. Tom can't cook.
> I can cook, **but** Tom can't.

B **Complete the questions and answers. Use *was, wasn't, were,* or *weren't*.**

1. _Was_____ Mei a doctor in China? Yes, she _____was_____.
2. _____ they in Hong Kong last month? No, they _____.
3. _____ Mr. Morris at work yesterday? No, he _____.
4. _____ you at home last Monday? No, we _____.
5. _____ the girls in Texas two weeks ago? Yes, they _____.

C **Match the questions and answers.**

__c_ 1. Where were Tad and Elena yesterday?   a. He was a mechanic.

____ 2. Was Elena a plumber in New York?   b. Julio and Elda were their friends.

____ 3. What was Tad's job five years ago?   c. They were at school.

____ 4. Who were their friends in Chile?   d. They were students in 2005.

____ 5. When were they students?   e. No, she wasn't.

D **Complete the story. Circle the correct words.**

Hector is (for /(from)) Mexico. He (lived / doesn't) there for forty years. He (was / were)
‌   1   2   3
a teacher in Mexico. He (was / can) teach math and computers. Hector (live / lives) in
‌   4   5
California now. He wants to teach, (but / ago) now he's studying English. He goes to
‌   6
English class (twice / three) times a week. His class in on Mondays, Wednesdays,
‌   7
(and / but) Fridays.
‌   8

2 Group work

A Work with 2–3 classmates. Choose 3 people from the picture on page 113. Write 2 sentences about each person's work experience. Talk about the sentences with your class.

The cook was a restaurant manager in Colombia.
He can cook, serve food, and manage a restaurant.

B Interview 3 classmates. Write their answers in your notebook.

ASK:

1. What was your job in your home country?
2. Do you have a job now?
3. Are you looking for a new job?

C Talk about the answers with your class.

> Classmate—Wen
> 1. He was a teacher.
> 2. No, he doesn't.
> 3. Yes, he is.

PROBLEM SOLVING

A Listen and read about Mrs. Galvan. What is her problem?

Mrs. Galvan moved to San Diego this week. She's looking for a job. She can work weekdays, but she can't work on weekends. Mrs. Galvan was a restaurant manager in Los Angeles. She can use a computer, cook, and serve food. Mrs. Galvan is worried. She needs to start work this week.

Food Server
PT, M–F 9:00–2:00
$5 per hour

Restaurant Manager
Nights and weekends
$18 per hour

Assistant Manager
FT, M–F 8:30 a.m.–4:30 p.m.
$12 per hour

B Work with your classmates. Look at the job ads and answer the question. (More than one answer is possible.)

What is the best job for Mrs. Galvan?

C Work with your classmates. Make a list of other jobs Mrs. Galvan can do.

UNIT 11

Safety First

FOCUS ON

• traffic signs
• safety at home and at work
• *should* and *shouldn't*
• 911 emergency calls
• traffic safety

LESSON 1 **Vocabulary**

1 Learn traffic signs

 A Look at the pictures. What colors, numbers, and words do you see?

 B Listen and look at the pictures.

 C Listen and repeat the words.

1. stop
2. road work
3. school crossing
4. no parking
5. no left turn
6. speed limit

D Look at the pictures. Complete the sentences.

1. The _____ no left turn _____ sign with the black arrow means you can't turn left.

2. There's a yellow _____ sign. Students can walk here.

3. The sign with the number gives the _____. Drive 35 miles per hour here.

4. There's a red _____ sign. You have to stop.

5. There's an orange _____ sign. People are working on the street.

6. The _____ sign with the "P" means you can't park here.

2 Talk about work safety

A Work with your classmates. Match the words with the pictures.

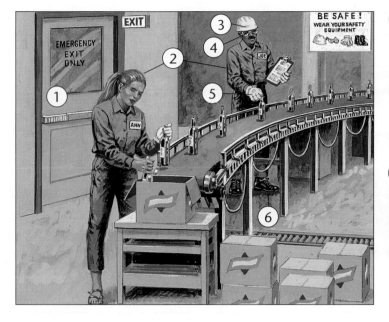

____ careful	____ factory workers	____ safety boots
____ careless	____ fire extinguisher	____ safety glasses
____ dangerous/unsafe	____ hard hat	____ safety gloves
_1_ emergency exit	____ safe	____ wet floor

STUDENT AUDIO

B Listen and check your answers. Then practice the words with a partner.

C Look at the factory workers. Match the names with the descriptions.

_b_ 1. Ann   a. He's careless. He doesn't see the wet floor.

____ 2. Joe   b. She's careless. She isn't wearing her safety boots.

____ 3. Tim   c. She's careful. She wears safety glasses and safety gloves.

____ 4. Tanya   d. He's careful. He's wearing safety glasses and safety gloves.

D Work with a partner. Ask and answer questions.
Talk about the factory workers in 2A.

A: Is Tanya careful or careless at work?

B: She's careful. She wears a hard hat. How about Tim?

A: He's careless. He doesn't wear safety boots.

TEST YOURSELF ✔

Close your book. Write 6 words for traffic signs and 4 words for safety
equipment. Check your spelling in a dictionary.

1 Read about safe and dangerous behavior

 A **Look at the pictures. Listen.**

B **Listen again. Read the sentences.**

1. I always drive fast. I never wear a seat belt. My friends worry, but I don't.
2. I always talk on my cell phone at work.
3. My co-workers say I should be careful, but I don't worry.
4. I never check the smoke detectors at home. My sister worries, but I don't.
5. My sister, my friends, and my co-workers worry too much. They should relax.
6. Oh, no! Here comes a police officer. Maybe I should worry now.

C **Check your understanding. Circle the correct words.**

1. Frank ((drives) / doesn't drive) fast.   3. Frank likes his (sofa / cell phone).
2. His friends (worry / don't worry).   4. Frank isn't (careful / careless).

2 Write about your behavior

A **Write your story. Complete the sentences.**

I _____ drive fast.

I _____ wear a seat belt.

I _____ talk on a cell phone at work or in the car.

I _____ check my smoke detector at home.

B **Read your story to a partner.**

> **Need help?**
>
> **Adverbs of frequency**
> always
> usually
> sometimes
> never

☑ Interpret and identify safe and unsafe behavior for accident prevention

3 Make a safety checklist

A Listen and complete the questions. Then check (✔) *Yes, I do.* or *No, I don't.*

Do you...	Yes, I do.	No, I don't.
1. always drive the ___speed limit___ ?	✔	
2. drive fast near _____?		
3. know where the emergency _____ are in the building?		
4. wear _____ equipment at work?		
5. have a _____ detector in the kitchen?		

Are you safe?

B Work with a partner. Talk about your safety habits at home, at work, and in the car. Use the chart.

A: *Do you wear safety equipment at work?*
B: *Yes, I always wear safety equipment. Do you?*

4 Real-life math

Read about the workers. Answer the questions.

Twenty-five of the one hundred workers at ABC Chemical Factory never wear their safety gloves. That means 25% never wear their gloves and 75% wear them.

Ten of the one hundred workers never wear their safety glasses.

1. What percent of the workers don't wear their safety glasses? _____%

2. What percent of the workers wear their safety glasses? _____%

Some workers at ABC Chemical Factory

TEST YOURSELF ✔

Close your book. Write 3 things you do to be safe at home, in the car, or at work. Talk about your ideas with the class.

1 Learn *should* and *should not*

A Look at the poster. Read the sentences. How can people be safe at home?

You should:	You should NOT:
 Know your neighbors. Lock doors and windows at night. Tell the manager about problems.	 Open the door to strangers. Leave the building door open. Walk alone in the parking lot at night.

B Study the charts. Complete the sentences below.

SHOULD AND *SHOULD NOT*

Statements					
I You He She	should	lock the door.	We You They	should	lock the door.

1. He ___Should___ lock the door.   2. We should ___lock___ the door.

Negative statements						Contractions
I You He She	should not	walk alone.	We You They	should not	walk alone.	should not = shouldn't You shouldn't walk alone.

3. She ___should not___ walk alone.   4. They _____ alone.

C Complete the sentences with *should* or *shouldn't*. Use the poster in 1A.
Read the sentences to a partner.

1. You _____shouldn't_____ leave the front door open.
2. You _____should_____ walk in the parking lot with other people.
3. You _____should_____ close the building door.
4. You _____shouldn't_____ open the door to strangers.

2 Ask and answer information questions with *should*

A Study the chart. Ask and answer the questions.

Information questions and answers with *should*

A: When should she walk with a friend?	**A:** What should they do?
B: She should walk with a friend at night.	**B:** They should lock the door.

B Match the questions with the answers.

___b___ 1. Sara has to walk home at night. What should she do?

___c___ 2. I don't understand. What should I do?

___e___ 3. Bob has a toothache. Where should he go?

___a___ 4. We are students. When should we study?

___d___ 5. Jen has a fever. What should she do?

a. We should study every day.

b. She should walk with a friend.

c. You should ask for help.

d. She should call the doctor.

e. He should go to the dentist.

3 Use *should* to talk about classroom rules

A Work with a partner. Answer the question.
What should students do in class?

B Work with a partner. Complete the poster below with the rules of your class.

Follow Classroom Rules! It's Easy!

Students should . . .	Students shouldn't . . .
1. speak English in class.	4. sleep in class.
2. _____.	5. _____.
3. _____.	6. _____.

TEST YOURSELF ✔

Close your book. Write 3 sentences about your school's safety rules.
Use *should* or *shouldn't*.

1 Learn to call 911

A Look at the pictures. Then answer the questions.

There's a traffic accident.

There's a robbery.

There's a

296

296 GREEN STREET

1. Who needs help?

2. What's the emergency?

3. Where's the emergency?

STUDENT AUDIO

B Listen and read.

A: 911. Emergency.
B: There's a fire at my neighbor's house.
A: What's the address?
B: It's 412 Oak Street.
A: Is anyone hurt?
B: I don't know.
A: OK. Help is on the way.

Is anyone hurt?

I don't know.

C Listen again and repeat.

D Work with a partner. Practice the conversation. Use emergencies from 1A.

A: 911. Emergency.
B: _____.
A: What's the address?
B: It's _____.
A: Is anyone hurt?
B: _____.
A: OK. _____ is on the way.

> **Need help?**
>
> **Help** is on the way.
> **A police officer** is on the way.
> **An ambulance** is on the way.
>
>

E **Listen and write the emergency information.**

1. What:	car accident		**3.** What:	
Where:	Pine Ave. and Hope St.		Where:	
Who needs help:	a man		Who needs help:	
2. What:			**4.** What:	
Where:			Where:	
Who needs help:			Who needs help:	

2 Practice your pronunciation

 A **Listen and point to the word you hear.**

should   shouldn't

 **B** **Listen for *should* or *shouldn't*. Circle *a* or *b*.**

1. a. should
   (b.) shouldn't
2. a. should
   b. shouldn't

3. a. should
   b. shouldn't
4. a. should
   b. shouldn't

5. a. should
   b. shouldn't
6. a. should
   b. shouldn't

C **Work with a partner. Read the sentences. Should you call 911?**
Check (✔) the correct boxes.

A: *I have a headache.*
B: *You shouldn't call 911.*

	Should	Shouldn't
1. I have a headache.		✔
2. My friend has a stomachache.		
3. There's a fire in the kitchen.		
4. I need a prescription.		
5. There's a bad car accident.		
6. There's a robbery.		

TEST YOURSELF ✔

Work with a partner. Partner A: Report an emergency. Partner B:
Ask for more information. Tell your partner that help is on the way.
Then change roles.

1 Get ready to read

A **Read the definitions.**

pull over: to drive the car to the side of the road and stop in a safe place

cause: to make something happen

B **Work with your classmates. Ask and answer the questions.**

1. Why do people have car accidents?
2. Why do people pull over?

pull over

2 Read about safe drivers

A **Read the article.**

Be Safe, Be Smart, Pull Over

angel *driving*

Unsafe drivers cause 50% of the car accidents in the U.S. every year. These drivers don't pay attention.[1] Be a safe driver. Pay attention to the road or pull over.

- Sometimes you have to read a map, but you shouldn't read and drive. You should **pull over**. *soldom* *sold*

- Sometimes you're tired, but you can't sleep and drive. **Pull over**!

- Do you have to use your cell phone in the car? Do you have to pay attention to your child? You should **pull over**.

- Don't forget! You have to **pull over** when you have a car accident. It's the law.

---

[1] pay attention – look, listen, and be careful

Source: *New York State DMV*

STUDENT AUDIO

B **Listen and read the article again.**

C Complete the sentences. Use the words in the box.

read a map	pull over	cell phone	unsafe drivers	~~pay attention~~

1. You should _____pay attention_____ when you are driving a car.
2. You shouldn't _____read a map_____ when you are driving.
3. You have to _____pull over_____ if you have an accident.
4. You should pull over to use a _____cell phone_____.
5. _____Unsafe drivers_____ cause 50% of traffic accidents.

D Read and check (✔) *yes* or *no*.

Should you pull over...	Yes	No
1. when you are tired?	✔	
2. when you see a stop sign?		✓
3. when you see a road work sign?	✓	
4. when you have to read a map?	✓	
5. when you have to use your cell phone?	✓	
6. when you have an accident?	✓	

sho

3 Learn about traffic accidents

A Look at the pie chart. Complete the sentences.

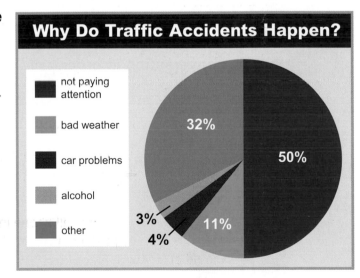

Why Do Traffic Accidents Happen?

- not paying attention
- bad weather
- car problems
- alcohol
- other

32%   50%   3%   4%   11%

1. _3_ % of car accidents happen because drivers drink _alcohol_.
2. _50_ % of car accidents happen because drivers aren't paying _attention_.
3. _11_ % of car accidents happen because of _bad_ weather.
4. _4_ % of car accidents happen because of car _problems_.

B Think about the question. Talk about the answer with your class.

What other things can cause accidents?

BRING IT TO LIFE

Watch the traffic in your neighborhood. Are the drivers paying attention? Tell your classmates about the drivers in your neighborhood.

1 Grammar

A Write the answers to the questions.

1. There's a school crossing sign. Should I slow down?
   Yes, you should.

2. Teo is driving to work. Should he wear his seat belt?
   Yes, he should

3. The floor is wet. Should Min and Janet walk on it?
   No, they shouldn't

4. I'm driving home, but I'm very tired. Should I pull over?
   Yes, you should

> **Grammar note**
>
> **Yes/No questions with *should***
>
> A: Should I call 911?
> B: Yes, you should. *or*
>   No, you shouldn't.
> A: Should he wear gloves?
> B: Yes, he should. *or*
>   No, he shouldn't.

B Match the questions with the answers.

_c_ 1. What's the emergency?   a. A man and a woman.

_e_ 2. What should I do?   b. 122 Pine Street.

_a_ 3. Who needs help?   c. There's a car accident.

_b_ 4. Where's the emergency?   d. No, they shouldn't.

_d_ 5. Should people drink and drive?   e. You should call 911.

C Put the conversation in order.

_4_ It's 2386 3rd Avenue.   _1_ 911. Emergency.   _3_ What's the address?

_5_ Help is on the way.   _2_ There's a fire.

D Look at the signs. Read the sentences. Write your advice.

1. Luis isn't paying attention.
   He should watch for children.

2. Anne is looking for a place to park.
   He should park

3. Ted is driving fifty-five miles per hour.
   He, shouldn't driving

4. Molly is driving and talking to her friend.
   He, should towing

2 Group work

A Work with 2–3 classmates. Look at the pictures on page 125.
Write 5 sentences with *should* or *shouldn't*.
Talk about the sentences with your class.

Ann should wear safety glasses. Tim shouldn't listen to music at work.

B Interview 3 classmates. Write their answers in your notebook.

ASK:

1. How often do you wear your seat belt?
2. Do you check your smoke detector batteries every 6 months?
3. How often do you wear safety glasses or gloves?

> Classmate—Lina
>
> 1. She always wears her seat belt.
> 2. Yes, she does.
> 3. She sometimes wears safety glasses.

C Talk about the answers with your class.

PROBLEM SOLVING

A Listen and read about Mr. Brown. What is his problem?

Mr. Brown is in the parking lot at the supermarket. He's very tired. He's parking his car and he doesn't see the car next to him! He has a small accident. He looks around the parking lot, but the driver of the other car is not there.

B Work with your classmates. Answer the question.
(More than one answer is possible.)

What should Mr. Brown do?
    a. Call the police.
    b. Call 911.
    c. Talk to the market manager.
    d. Other: _____

C Work with your classmates. Write a note that Mr. Brown can put on the car for the driver.

Free Time

FOCUS ON
- weather and seasons
- leisure activities
- the future with *be going to*
- making future plans
- holidays

LESSON 1 Vocabulary

1 Learn weather words and holidays

A Look at the pictures. When are the holidays?

STUDENT AUDIO **B** Listen and look at the pictures.

STUDENT AUDIO **C** Listen and repeat the words.

   1. snowing   2. raining   3. cloudy   4. sunny   5. hot   6. cold

D Look at the pictures. Complete the sentences.

1. It's _____hot_____ this Independence Day.
2. It's _____cold_____ this Thanksgiving.
3. It's _____sunny_____ this Father's Day.
4. It's _____snowing_____ this New Year's Day.
5. It's _____cloudy_____ this Mother's Day.
6. It's _____raining_____ this Presidents' Day.

2 Talk about leisure activities

A Work with your classmates. Match the words with the pictures.

<u>7</u> go out to eat   <u>8</u> go to the movies   <u>4</u> play soccer

<u>6</u> go swimming   <u>3</u> have a picnic   <u>1</u> stay home

<u>5</u> go to the beach   <u>2</u> make a snowman

B Listen and check your answers. Then practice the words with a partner.

C Look at the pictures. Circle the correct words.

1. In the winter, it's (**cold** / hot). They like to (play soccer / **stay home**).
2. The flowers are beautiful in the (fall / **spring**). They like to have (movies / **picnics**).
3. The weather is (**hot** / cold) in the summer. They like to (**go** / stay) to the beach.
4. In the fall, they like to go (**out to eat** / to the beach). Other people like to go
   (swimming / **to the movies**).

D Work with a partner. Ask and answer the questions.

1. What is your favorite time of the year?
2. What do you like to do at that time of the year?

TEST YOURSELF ✔

Close your book. Write your 5 favorite activities for hot and cold weather.
Check your spelling in a dictionary.

1 Read about a trip to a baseball game

STUDENT
AUDIO

 A Look at the pictures. Listen.

STUDENT
AUDIO

B Listen again. Read the sentences.

1. I can't wait for the weekend. I don't have to work or go to school on Saturdays or Sundays.
2. On Saturdays, I have fun with my son.
3. This Saturday, we're going to see a baseball game.
4. We're going to watch the game and eat hot dogs.
5. My son wants to catch a ball at the game.

C Check your understanding. Circle *a* or *b*.

1. He _____ on Saturday.
   a. works
   b. doesn't work
2. They're going to see a baseball game _____.
   a. on Saturday
   b. on Sunday
3. He's going to see the game with his _____.
   a. boss
   b. son
4. His son wants to catch a _____ at the game.
   a. ball
   b. hot dog

2 Write about your plans

A Write your story. Complete the sentences.

I can't wait for _the weekend_.

I don't _____ on _____.

On _Saturdays_, I'm going to _~~shop~~_.

B Read your story to a partner.

3 Use a bus schedule to plan a trip

A Listen to the conversation. Complete the schedule below.

Metro Bus West Line—Weekend Schedule

	Grant Street	Front St. School	Town Mall	Riverside Baseball Stadium	City Park
Bus #1	8:00	8:15	8:30	8:45	9:00
Bus #2	12:00	12:15	12:30	12:45	1:00
Bus #3	4:00	4:15	4:30	4:45	5:00

B Match the questions with the answers.

Pedro and his son have to get on the bus at Grant Street. The baseball game is at 1:00.

_b_ 1. What bus do they have to take?   a. 12:45

_c_ 2. How many stops are between Grant Street and the stadium? b. Bus #2

_d_ 3. What time do they have to take the bus? c. two

_a_ 4. What time will they stop at the stadium? d. 12:00

C Work with a partner. Practice the conversation. Use the bus schedule in 3A.

You are on Grant Street.

A: Excuse me, I have to be at the mall at 5:00. Can I take the bus from here?

B: Yes. Take the number 3 bus at 4:00.

A: Thank you.

TEST YOURSELF ✔

Close your book. Write 3 sentences about places you are going to go this weekend.

I'm going to go to the mall this weekend.

1 Learn the future with *be going to*

A Look at the pictures. What season is it?

It's going to be sunny on Friday.

It's going to be cloudy on Saturday.

It's going to rain on Sunday.

B Study the charts. Complete the sentences below.

THE FUTURE WITH *BE GOING TO*

Statements							
I	am	going to	have a picnic.	We	are	going to	have a picnic.
You	are			You			
He She	is			They			
It	is	going to	be sunny.				

1. She is _going to_ have a picnic.

2. They _are_ going _to_ have a picnic.

Negative statements							
I	am	not going to	have a picnic.	We	are	not going to	have a picnic.
You	are			You			
He She	is			They			
It	is	not going to	be sunny.				

3. I am _not_ going to have a picnic.

4. We are not _going to_ have a picnic.

C Look at the pictures in 1A. Match the parts of the sentences.

_b_ 1. They are going to   a. rain on Saturday.

_d_ 2. It is going to   b. have a picnic on Friday.

_c_ 3. They are not going to   c. stay home on Saturday.

_a_ 4. It is not going to   d. rain on Sunday.

✔ Use the future with *be going to* to describe weather and future plans

2 Ask and answer questions with *be going to*

A Study the chart. Ask and answer the questions.

Information questions with *be going to*	
A: What are you going to do tonight? **B:** I'm going to study.	**A:** What are we going to do next week? **B:** We're going to (go to) Mexico.
A: What is he going to do tomorrow? **B:** He's going to see a movie.	**A:** What are they going to do next year? **B:** They're going to buy a house.

B Write the questions.

1. _What is she going to do tonight?_   She's going to watch TV tonight.
2. _____ I'm going to have a picnic on Saturday.
3. _____ We're going to have fun this weekend.
4. _____ They're going to study tomorrow.
5. _____ He's going to feed the dog tonight.

3 Practice questions with *be going to*

A Complete the questions. Use the words in the box. Then write your answers.

What   Who   When   ~~Where~~

1. _Where_____ are you going to go after class?
   _I'm going to go home._____

2. _____ are you going to do tomorrow?

   _____

3. _____ are you going to see a movie?

   _____

4. _____ are you going to talk to after class?

   _____

B Ask and answer the questions in 3A with a partner. Then write sentences about your partner's answers.

Juan is going to go to work.

TEST YOURSELF ✔

Close your book. Write 2 sentences about your future plans and 2 sentences about your partner's future plans.

I'm going to study tomorrow. Juan is going to go to work.

1 Plan to see a movie

A Read the movie ads. Say the titles and the times of the movies.

TOWN MALL THEATER

Where's the **MONEY?!** PG
Times: 5:30*, 8:00
Running Time: 90 minutes
$9.00 Adults $6.50 Children

THE ACTION MAN PG-13
Times: 6:00*, 8:45
Running Time: 120 minutes
$9.00 Adults $6.50 Children

RAIN IN MY EYES R
Times: 9:30
Running Time: 120 minutes
$9.00 Adults

My Friend **GREEN GEORGE** G
Family night special!
Times: 4:00*, 6:00*, 7:30
Running Time: 75 minutes
$9.00 Adults $6.50 Children

Bargain matinee show times 4:00–6:30. All tickets $6.00.

B Listen and read.

A: What are we going to do tonight?

B: Let's see a movie. *The Action Man* is playing at 6:00.

A: OK. How much are tickets?

B: The 6:00 show is only $6.00.

A: $6.00? That's a bargain. Let's go!

C Listen again and repeat.

D Work with a partner. Practice the conversation. Use the movie ads in 1A.

A: What are we _going to_ do tonight?

B: _Let's_ see a movie? _Rain in my_ is playing at _9:30_.

A: Sure. How much are _tickets_? _eyes_

B: _The 9:30_ show is only $6.00

A: _$9.00? That's_? Let's go!
cheat.

E Listen to the conversation. Answer the questions.

1. What movie are they going to see? _____Rain in My Eyes_____

2. What time are they going to meet? _____9:00_____

3. What time is the movie? _____9:30_____

4. Can they take the bus? _____Yes____ 9:00____

sten to the sentences. What is different in the "relaxed"
onunciation?

	Formal	Relaxed
1. going to	A: What are we **going to** do today? B: We're **going to** go to the park.	A: What are we **going to** do today? B: We're **going to** go to the park.
2. want to	A: Do you **want to** go to a movie? B: Yes. I **want to** go to a movie.	A: Do you **want to** go to a movie? B: Yes. I **want to** go to a movie.

nd circle *formal* or *relaxed*.

relaxed

relaxed

relaxed

relaxed

relaxed

a partner. Read the questions and answers in 2A.

th

r classmates. Use the running times in the movie ads in 1A
questions.

going to see *Rain in My Eyes* at 9:30.
take the 11:15 bus home?

_____.

ng to take her children to see *My Friend, Green George* at 6:00.
n minutes from the movie theater. Can they be home at 7:30?

_____.

OURSELF ✔
th a partner. Use the movie ads in 1A to make plans this weekend.
: Name a movie you want to see. Partner B: Ask about the times
t prices. Then change roles.

1 Get ready to read

A **Read the definitions.**

occasion: a holiday, birthday, or other special day
greeting cards: cards for holidays, birthdays, and other
special occasions

B **Work with your classmates. Can you name the month for each h**

2 Read about greeting cards

A **Read the article.**

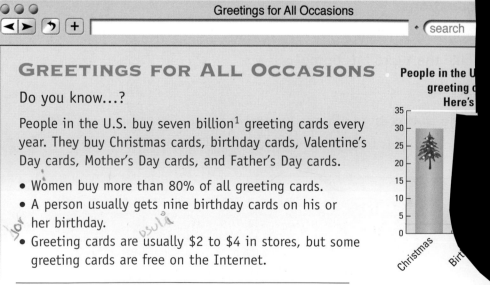

○ ○ ○   Greetings for All Occasions

◀▶ ↺ +   ◆ search

GREETINGS FOR ALL OCCASIONS

People in the U
greeting
Here's

Do you know...?

People in the U.S. buy seven billion[1] greeting cards every
year. They buy Christmas cards, birthday cards, Valentine's
Day cards, Mother's Day cards, and Father's Day cards.

- Women buy more than 80% of all greeting cards.
- A person usually gets nine birthday cards on his or
  her birthday.
- Greeting cards are usually $2 to $4 in stores, but some
  greeting cards are free on the Internet.

35
30
25
20
15
10
5
0

Christmas   Birt

[1]billion = 1,000,000,000

Source: www

STUDENT AUDIO

B **Listen and read the article again.**

C Complete the sentences. Use the words in the box.

| holidays   birthday   ~~greeting cards~~   Internet |

1. Americans buy seven billion ___greeting cards___ every year.
2. People buy greeting cards for birthdays and ___holidays___.
3. Some greeting cards are free on the ___Internet___.
4. A person usually gets nine greeting cards on his or her ___birthday___.

D Read the sentences. Write the answers.

1. Name three occasions when people buy greeting cards. _____
2. Name two places you can buy or get greeting cards. _____

3 Learn to use a phone book

A Look at the phone book. Answer the questions.

▶ **Holiday/Party Supply Stores**
BALLOONS AND THINGS ············· 555-2759 *(see our display ad this page)*
Hall's Card Shop ···················· 555-0225
Nancy's Cards and Gifts ·········· 555-7730
Paul's Flowers ····················· 555-3151
SPECIAL MOMENTS GIFTS ·········· 555-1351 *(see our display ad this page)*

HAPPY BIRTHDAY
BALLOONS AND THINGS
All your party decorations here!
Open 9:00 a.m.—8:00 p.m.
7 days

Special Moments Gifts
Birthdays!
Anniversaries! Valentine's Day
Something for everyone.
Open 9—9. Closed on Sundays
10% OFF THE PRICE WITH THIS AD

1. What's the phone number for Hall's Card Shop? ___The phone number is 555-0225.___
2. Where can you shop for flowers? ___Paul's Flowers 555-3151___
3. What time does Balloons and Things open every day? ___Open 9:00 am___
4. Where can you get 10% off the price of gifts? ___Special moments Gifts___
5. What store is closed on Sunday? ___Special moments Gifts___

B Think about the questions. Talk about the answers with your class.

1. What information can you find in the phone book?
2. What are some other ways to find information about places in your city?

BRING IT TO LIFE

Look in the phone book. Is there a holiday or greeting card store near your home? Bring the address to class.

1 Grammar

A Circle *a* or *b*.

1. Was it cloudy yesterday?
   a. Yes, it was.
   b. No, it isn't.
2. Is it raining today?
   a. Yes, it was.
   b. No, it isn't.
3. Is it going to snow tomorrow?
   a. Yes, it was.
   b. No, it isn't.
4. Was it hot yesterday?
   a. Yes, it was.
   b. No, it isn't.

> **Grammar note**
>
> **Questions with *be***
>
> **Present**
> A: Is it sunny today?
> B: Yes, it is. *or*
>   No, it isn't.
>
> **Past**
> A: Was it sunny yesterday?
> B: Yes, it was. *or*
>   No, it wasn't.
>
> **Future**
> A: Is it going to be sunny tomorrow?
> B: Yes, it is. *or*
>   No, it isn't.

B Match the questions with the answers.

_d_ 1. Is it going to be sunny tomorrow?   a. He's going to work.

____ 2. Is Joe going to study this evening?   b. Yes, he is.

____ 3. What's he going to do tomorrow?   c. No, I'm not.

____ 4. Are you going to cook next weekend?   d. Yes, it is.

C Unscramble the sentences.

1. next / be / going to / It's / cloudy / week _It's going to be cloudy next week._

2. this / going to / He's / at home / be / evening _____.

3. They're / going to / test / next / have / a / Friday _____.

4. tomorrow / are / What / going to / do / you _____?

D Complete the story. Use the words in the box.

| going   it's   clean   be   ~~is~~   sleep   Sunday   to |

Max _____is_____ listening to the weather report for the weekend. It's going to
             1

_____ sunny on Saturday. Max is _____ to have a picnic. It's going _____
      2   3   4

rain on Sunday morning. Max is going to stay in bed and _____. _____ going
                                                               5   6

to be cloudy on _____ afternoon. Max is going to _____ the house.
                       7   8

2 Group work

A Work with 2–3 classmates. Write 5 questions and answers about the pictures on page 137. Use *be going to.* Talk about the sentences with your class.

What are they going to do this summer?
They're going to go to the beach.

B Interview 3 classmates. Write their answers in your notebook.

ASK:

1. Are you going to see your friends this weekend?
2. Are you going to go to a party this weekend?
3. What are you going to do on Sunday?

> *Classmate #1 —Ben*
> *1. Yes, he is.*
> *2. No, he isn't.*
> *3. He's going to go to the library.*

C Talk about the answers with the class.

PROBLEM SOLVING

A Listen and read about Linda. What is her problem?

Linda lives in Chicago. Every year she drives two hours to her brother's house on Thanksgiving Day. Tomorrow is Thanksgiving. Linda is cooking and listening to the radio. The radio says that it's going to snow all night tonight and all day tomorrow. Linda doesn't like to drive in bad weather.

B Work with your classmates. Answer the question. (More than one answer is possible.)

What should Linda do?
    a. Drive to her brother's house now.
    b. Stay home and watch TV.
    c. Take the bus to her brother's house.
    d. Other: _____

C Work with your classmates. What should Linda tell her brother? Write 3 sentences.

THE FIRST STEP: Names and Numbers

Pg. 2 Exercise 1C

M = Man, W = Woman
1. W: Maria. M-A-R-I-A.
2. M: Lee. L-E-E.
3. W: Tom. T-O-M.
4. M: Rebecca. R-E-B-E-C-C-A.
5. W: Kumar. K-U-M-A-R.
6. M: David. D-A-V-I-D.

Pg. 3 Exercise 3C

M = Man, W = Woman
1. W: Twenty
2. M: Forty
3. W: Ninety
4. M: One hundred

UNIT 1   In the Classroom

Pg. 4 Lesson 1—Exercise 1B

M = Man, W = Woman
1. W: Listen to the letter "A."
2. M: Point to the letter "B."
3. W: Say the letter "C."
4. M: Repeat the letter "D."
5. W: Open the notebook.
6. M: Close the book.
7. W: Sit down, please.
8. M: Stand up, please.

Pg. 5 Lesson 1—Exercise 2B

M = Man, W = Woman, N = Narrator
1. W: What is it?
   M: It's a board. This is a white board. There are numbers on the white board today.
   N: board
2. M: Who is he?
   W: He's a teacher, Mr. Terrel. He's a good teacher.
   N: teacher
3. M: What is it?
   W: It's a clock. The clock is on the wall. It is 10:00.
   N: clock
4. W: Who are they?
   M: They're students. There are two students.
   N: students
5. M: What is it?
   W: It's a dictionary. The dictionary is open.
   N: dictionary
6. W: What are they?
   M: They're notebooks. There are three red notebooks.
   N: notebooks
7. M: What are they?
   W: They're pens. There are five blue pens.
   N: pens
8. W: What is it?
   M: It's a desk. There are many things on the desk.
   N: desk
9. W: What are they?
   M: They're books. There are four books.
   N: books
10. M: What are they?
    W: They are chairs. The chairs are black. They're two black chairs.
    N: chairs

Pg. 6 Lesson 2—Exercise 1A

S = Woman school clerk, J = Jim Santos
S: Tell me your first name.
J: Jim.
S: Please spell your last name.
J: S-A-N-T-O-S.
S: Complete the form. Please print your address.
J: OK.
S: Write your telephone number with the area code. Then write your email address. Sign your name on line five. Please give me the form. Welcome to school.

Pg. 7 Lesson 2—Exercise 3A

W = Woman, M = Man
1. W: Circle the last name.
2. M: Circle the telephone number.
3. W: Circle the area code.
4. M: Circle the email address.
5. W: Circle the first name.
6. M: Circle the signature.

Pg. 7 Lesson 2—Exercise 3B

W = Woman, M = Man
1. W: Print your first name.
2. M: Write your telephone number.
3. W: Print your last name.
4. M: Write your address.
5. W: Sign your name.
6. M: Write your area code.

Pg. 11 Lesson 4—Exercise 2B

W = Woman, M = Man
1. W: What is your name?
2. M: I'm John.
3. M: Who's your teacher?
4. W: My teacher is Carol Brown.
5. M: What's your name?

UNIT 2   My Classmates

Pg. 16 Lesson 1—Exercise 1B

W = Woman, M = Man
1. W: What time is it?
   M: It's eight o'clock in the morning. Jun is at home.
2. M: What time is it?
   W: It's nine fifteen a.m. Jun's at work.
3. W: What time is it?
   M: It's noon. Time for lunch.

4. M: What time is it?
   W: It's eight thirty p.m. He's at school.
5. W: What time is it?
   M: It's nine forty-five. Jun's at home.
6. M: What time is it?
   W: It's midnight. Jun's at home.

Pg. 17 Lesson 1—Exercise 2B

W = Woman, M = Man, N = Narrator
1. W: The month is March.
   N: month
2. W: What is the first day of the work week?
   M: Monday is the first day.
   N: day
3. W: The date for my first English class is March 8th, 2007.
   M: 3/8/07 is the date.
   N: date
4. M: One week is seven days. The week is from Sunday to Saturday.
   N: week
5. M: What day was yesterday?
   W: Yesterday was Monday, March 5th.
   N: yesterday
6. M: What day is today?
   W: Today is March 6th. It's a beautiful day today.
   N: today
7. W: Tomorrow is March 7th.
   M: I'll see you tomorrow.
   N: tomorrow
8. M: How many months are in a year?
   W: There are twelve months in a year.
   N: year

Pg. 19 Lesson 2—Exercise 3A

W1 = Woman 1, W2 = Woman 2, M1 = Man 1,
M2 = Man 2
1. W1: What's your name?
   M1: My name is James. That's J-A-M-E-S.
   W1: Where are you from?
   M1: I'm from China.
2. M1: What's your name?
   W1: My name is Lan. That's L-A-N.
   M1: Where are you from?
   W1: I'm from Vietnam.
3. M2: What's your name?
   W2: My name is Linda. That's L-I-N-D-A.
   M2: Where are you from?
   W2: I'm from Mexico.
4. W2: What's your name?
   M2: My name is Pedro. That's P-E-D-R-O.
   W2: Where are you from?
   M2: I'm from the Philippines.

Pg. 19 Lesson 2—Exercise 3B

W = Woman, M = Man
1. W: What's your name?
2. M: Where are you from?
3. W: What's your date of birth?
4. M: What's your favorite color?

Pg. 23 Lesson 4—Exercise 1E

M = Man, W = Woman, W2 = Woman 2, A = Announcer
1. M: What's your name?
   W: Pat Tyson. Mrs. Pat Tyson.
   M: Nice to meet you, Mrs. Tyson.
2. M: Good evening. I'm Pat Song. Welcome to class.
   W: Good evening, Mr. Song.
3. M: I have an appointment with Ms. Terry Miller.
   W: Yes. Ms. Miller can see you now.
4. W: Excuse me. My registration form says my teacher is Mrs. Terry Farmer.
   W2: I'm Mrs. Farmer. Welcome to class.
5. W: Hello. I'm Jean Silver.
   W2: Hello, Ms. Silver. Nice to meet you.
6. A: Attention! Paging Mr. Gold. Paging Mr. Gene Gold. Please come to the office. You have a phone call.

Pg. 23 Lesson 4—Exercise 2B

M = Man, W = Woman
W: OK, Mr. Milovich. I need to complete this form with you. Let's see, the date today is October 26th, 2007. Let me write that down…ten, twenty-six, oh-seven. What is your first name?
M: My first name is Sasha. That's S-A-S-H-A. Sasha.
W: OK. Are you married or single?
M: I'm single.
W: OK. Single. Let's see. What's your date of birth?
M: My date of birth is June 10th, 1971.
W: That's 6/10/71. Alright. Where are you from, Mr. Milovich?
M: I'm from Russia.
W: What's your address?
M: It's 1769 Rose Avenue, Chicago, Illinois, 60601.
W: What's your phone number?
M: My phone number is area code three one two, five five five, one six six nine.
W: Did you say three one two, five five five, one six six nine?
M: Yes, that's right.

UNIT 3   Family and Friends

Pg. 28 Lesson 1—Exercise 1B

M = Man, W = Woman, W2 = Woman 2, A = Announcer
A: The Martinez family.
1. W: This picture is from June 22nd, 1997. Carlos and Anita are married. It's their wedding day.
   M: Carlos is a new husband today. He is very happy to be a husband.
2. W2: Anita is his new wife. She is happy to be a wife.
   W: This picture is from November 15th, 1999. That's Carlos and Eric.
3. M: Carlos is a father today. He's a little nervous about being a father.
4. W2: Eric is his new son. Eric's a beautiful boy.
   W: This picture is from April 20th, 2003.
5. W2: Anita is a wonderful mother.
6. W: Her new daughter is Robin. She's a beautiful girl.
   W2: This is a photograph of the Martinez family on June 30th, 2006.

7. M: Carlos and Anita are busy parents. Soon they'll be very busy parents.
8. W: Eric and Robin are the only two children in this picture. Soon there will be three children.

Pg. 29 Lesson 1—Exercise 2B

E = Eric (age 10), N = Narrator
   E: Hi. I'm Eric and this is my family. They are all great people.
1. E: These are my grandparents. They are the best grandparents in the world.
   N: grandparents
2. E: This is my grandmother. Her name is Helen, but I call her Grandma. She's a really great grandmother.
   N: grandmother
3. E: My grandfather is Ramiro. We play together a lot. My grandfather is really funny.
   N: grandfather
4. E: My parents are Carlos and Anita, but they are Mom and Dad to me. I love my parents very much.
   N: parents
5. E: Hector is my uncle. Uncle Hector and my dad are brothers.
   N: uncle
6. E: That's my aunt. Her name is Sue. Aunt Sue makes the best chocolate cake.
   N: aunt
7. E: This is Robin. She is my sister. She's a good little sister—most of the time.
   N: sister
8. E: This is my new brother. He's one year old. My brother's name is Jimmy.
   N: brother
9. E: I have a cousin. Her name is Sandra. I visit my cousin every Sunday.
   N: cousin

Pg. 31 Lesson 2—Exercise 3A

M = Man, W = Woman
1. M: Simon is Paulina's husband. He is the man with gray hair and brown eyes.
2. W: Karina is Paulina's daughter. She is the girl with brown hair and blue eyes.
3. M: Sam is Paulina's son. He is the boy with blond hair and brown eyes.

Pg. 34 Lesson 4—Exercise 1A

W = Woman
   W: Today is March 1st. March is my favorite month. There are a lot of special days in March. Look at my calendar. March 2nd is my friend Ashley's birthday. The first day of spring is March 20th. My friend Julie's birthday is on March 23rd.

Pg. 35 Lesson 4—Exercise 2A

M = Man, W = Woman
1. Digital answering machine voice: October 5th, 3:00 p.m.
   M: Hi. It's me, Tim. Please call me at 555-9241. I'll be here all afternoon. Again, that's 5-5-5, 9-2-4-1.

2. Digital answering machine voice: February 21st, 9:45 a.m.
   W: Hello, Martha. It's Jackie calling. It's about 9:45 on February 21st. I just wanted to say, "Happy Birthday." Hope you are having a great day. Call me if you can. 555-7737. That's 5-5-5, 7-7-3-7.
3. Digital answering machine voice: May 18th, 7:30 p.m.
   M: This is Jim calling. My number is 5-5-5, 1-0-8-9. It's about 7:30 in the evening, Friday, May 18th. Are you there? Hello? Hello? Hello? OK. See you Monday.

Pg. 35 Lesson 4—Exercise 3B

M = Man, W = Woman
1. F: Teresa's birthday is January third.
2. M: My birthday is July twenty-sixth.
3. F: Armando's birthday is October seventh.
4. M: My mother's birthday is April fourteenth.
5. F: My birthday is September first.
6. M: My daughter's birthday is August twenty-third.

UNIT 4   At Home

Pg. 40 Lesson 1—Exercise 1B

M = Man, M2 = Man 2, W = Woman, W2 = Woman 2
1. W: Is the bathroom pink?
   W2: Yes, it is. The bathroom is a very pretty pink.
2. M: Is the bedroom brown?
   M2: No, it isn't. The bedroom is blue.
3. W: What color is the garage?
   M: The garage is gray.
4. M: What color is the living room?
   M2: The living room is green.
5. W: What color is the dining area?
   W2: The dining area is yellow.
6. M: Is the kitchen green or white?
   W: The kitchen is white.

Pg. 41 Lesson 1—Exercise 2B

L = Lisa, K = Ken, N = Narrator
L: Hi, I'm Lisa. I live in an apartment on the second floor. I really like my apartment.
1. L: Here's the bedroom. This is my dresser. It's new.
   N: dresser
2. L: Look at my bookcase. I have many books in the bookcase.
   N: bookcase
3. L: Here's my bed. The bed is new, too.
   N: bed
4. L: Here's the bathroom. Look at the sink. The bathroom sink is new.
   N: sink
5. L: The bathtub is great. It's a big, old bathtub.
   N: bathtub
   K: Hello. My name is Ken. My apartment is on the first floor.
6. K: There's my living room. My sofa looks good there. It's a comfortable sofa.
   N: sofa

7. K: Do you see that chair? It's my favorite chair for reading.
   N: chair
8. K: The living room rug is old. Maybe I'll get a new rug soon.
   N: rug
9. K: My TV is perfect there. I like to watch TV.
   N: TV
10. K: I spend a lot of time in the kitchen. That's my kitchen table. I eat and do homework at that table.
    N: table
11. K: I like the stove. It's a gas stove.
    N: stove
12. K: The refrigerator is nice, too. It's a big refrigerator.
    N: refrigerator

Pg. 43 Lesson 2—Exercise 3A

T = Tina, S = Sally
T: Sally, how about this TV? It's perfect for our house.
S: No, this TV is so small. Look at that TV! It's big. It's beautiful. It's perfect for our apartment.
T: Ummm...are you sure?
S: Tina, look at these chairs. They look comfortable and brown is a great color.
T: No, these chairs are terrible! Look at those chairs. They're beautiful. Green is my favorite color. They're perfect for our place.
S: Uhhhhh...are you sure?

Pg. 46 Lesson 4—Exercise 1B

M1 = Man 1, M2 = Man 2, M3 = Man 3, M4 = Man 4,
W1 = Woman 1, W2 = Woman 2, W3 = Woman 3,
W4 = Woman 4
1. M1: Please pay the gas bill today. It's seventeen dollars.
   W1: Seventeen dollars? That's not bad.
2. W2: What's the date?
   M2: It's September 29th.
   W2: Oh! Don't forget to pay the phone bill. It's twenty-six dollars.
   M2: Yes, dear. Twenty-six dollars. I'm paying it right now.
3. M3: When is the electric bill due?
   W3: It's due on October 1st. Please pay it. It's eighty-two dollars.
   M3: Eighty-two dollars? That's a lot of money.
4. M4: Is today the 14th?
   W4: Yes, it is. We need to pay the water bill. It's fourteen dollars and fifty cents and it's due tomorrow.
   M4: Fourteen fifty? OK, I can pay it tomorrow morning.

UNIT 5 In the Neighborhood

Pg. 52 Lesson 1—Exercise 1B

M1 = Man 1, M2 = Man 2, W1 = Woman 1,
W2 = Woman 2
1. W1: Excuse me, where's the school?
   M1: The high school is on 2nd Street.

2. M1: Is there a supermarket on 2nd Street?
   W1: Yes, there's a supermarket on 2nd Street.
3. M1: Excuse me, where's the hospital? I think I'm lost.
   M2: The hospital is on Elm Street between 2nd and 3rd.
4. W1: Is there a bank nearby?
   W2: Yes. The bank is on Oak Street on the corner of 1st and Oak.
5. M1: Can you tell me where the fire station is?
   W1: No problem. The fire station is on 1st Street.
6. M1: Can I help you?
   W1: Yes, please. Where is the police station?
   M1: The police station is on Pine Street.

Pg. 53 Lesson 1—Exercise 2B

M = Man, N = Narrator
M: Hello. My name is Mark. I live in Riverside. This is my neighborhood.
1. M: I go to the supermarket every Monday. Fast Mart is a good supermarket.
   N: supermarket
2. M: The pharmacy is on the corner. When I need medicine, I go to the pharmacy.
   N: pharmacy
3. M: I go to the movies every Friday. Tonight I'm going to see *Hometown Friends* at the movie theater.
   N: movie theater
4. M: The car on the street is blue. That's my friend Sam driving the car.
   N: car
5. M: There's a stop sign on the corner. Don't forget to stop at the stop sign!
   N: stop sign
6. M: Here comes the school bus. The children are riding the bus to school.
   N: bus
7. M: A girl is waiting at the bus stop. She goes to the bus stop every morning at 7:45.
   N: bus stop
8. M: Bob's Restaurant is my favorite restaurant in town!
   N: restaurant
9. M: The gas station is near the park. I work at that gas station.
   N: gas station
10. M: The parking lot is over there. There is one parking lot on this street.
    N: parking lot
11. M: Town Savings is my bank. It's a good bank.
    N: bank
12. M: There's a boy riding a bicycle. Do you like to ride a bicycle?
    N: bicycle

Pg. 55 Lesson 2—Exercise 3A

M1 = Man 1, M2 = Man 2, M3 = Man 3, M4 = Man 4,
M5 = Man 5, W1= Woman 1, W2 = Woman 2,
W3 = Woman 3, W4 = Woman 4, W5 = Woman 5
1. W1: Excuse me, where's the parking lot?
   M1: It's behind the pharmacy.

2. M2: (Sneezing) Excuse me. Where is the clinic?
   W2: The clinic is between the parking lot and the apartment building.
3. W3: Where's the supermarket?
   M3: It's in front of the apartment building.
4. M4: Excuse me. Is there a hospital on Lee Street?
   W4: Yes, it's across from the pharmacy.
5. W5: Is there a fire station on this street?
   M5: Yes. The fire station is next to the post office.

Pg. 58 Lesson 4—Exercise 1B

W = Woman
W: 1. Let me give you directions to the clinic from here. Go straight on Grand Avenue.
   2. Turn right on 12th Street.
   3. Go two blocks on Maple Street.
   4. Turn left on 14th Street.
   5. It's across from the park.
   6. It's next to the pharmacy.

UNIT 6   Daily Routines

Pg. 64 Lesson 1—Exercise 1B

M = Man, W = Woman
M: Good morning! My name's Brian.
W: And I'm Jen.
M: This is our daily routine.
1. M: In the morning, we get up at 7 a.m.
   W: Yes. We get up at 7:00.
2. W: We get dressed at 7:15.
   M: Uh-huh. 7:15 is when we get dressed.
3. M: At 7:30 we eat breakfast.
   W: That's right. Before we go to work, we eat breakfast.
4. W: In the evening, we come home at 5:30.
   M: It's nice to come home together.
5. W: We make dinner at 6:00.
   M: Yes, we make dinner together.
6. W: We usually go to bed at 11:00 p.m. Right, honey?
   M: Yes, that's right. We go to bed at 11:00.
   M and W: That's it. That's our daily routine!

Pg. 65 Lesson 1—Exercise 2B

W = Woman, N = Narrator
1. W: On school days, Deka and her friend walk to school together. They practice English while they walk.
   N: walk to school
2. W: After class, Deka and her friends have lunch. They usually have lunch in the cafeteria.
   N: have lunch
3. W: Deka has to ride the bus for 15 minutes. She likes to ride the bus to her job.
   N: ride the bus
4. W: Deka works at a supermarket. She has to work there Monday through Friday.
   N: work
5. W: In the evening, Deka has to do housework. She likes to do housework.
   N: do housework

6. W: When the house is clean, she takes a shower. She likes to take a hot shower and relax.
   N: take a shower
7. W: Deka drinks coffee to stay awake. She likes to drink coffee.
   N: drink coffee
8. W: Deka thinks that doing homework is very important. At the end of the day, Deka has time to do homework.
   N: do homework
9. W: Deka is tired after a long day. At midnight, it's time for her to go to bed.
   N: go to bed

Pg. 67 Lesson 2—Exercise 3A

MB = Mel Brown
Mel: I'm Mel. I work at Joe's Market and I like my job a lot. Joe's is a small market in my neighborhood. I work on Monday, Wednesday, and Friday from 10:00 in the morning to 3:00 in the afternoon. In the morning, I mop the floor and wash the windows. In the afternoon, I help the manager and answer the phone. The hours are good and the people are nice. It's a great job for me.

Pg. 71 Lesson 4—Exercise 1E

M = Man, W = Woman, W1 = Woman 1, W2 = Woman 2
1. M: Excuse me. The copy machine is out of paper. Can you help me?
   W: Sure. You need to fill the machine. Put the paper here.
   M: Oh, that's easy. Thanks for your help.
2. W: I think the printer is broken. It doesn't print.
   M: No, it's OK. Just turn on the printer. Push this button.
   W: Oops! My mistake. I'll turn it on.
3. M: Excuse me. The stapler is empty. Do you have another one?
   W: No, let's fill the stapler. Put the staples here.
   M: OK. Thanks.
4. W1: Excuse me, Mrs. Blake. Can you help me? How do you turn off the computer?
   W2: Push this button.
   W1: Oh! OK, thank you.

UNIT 7   Shop and Spend

Pg. 76 Lesson 1, Exercise 1B

M1 = Man 1, M2 = Man 2, W1 = Woman 1,
W2 = Woman 2, B1 = Boy 1, B2 = Boy 2
1. W1: Can I have a penny? I need to buy a one-cent stamp.
   M1: Sure. Here's a penny.
2. B1: Can I have a nickel? I want some gum.
   W2: Yes, honey. Here's a nickel.
3. B1: Candy is 10 cents. I need a dime.
   B2: Here's a dime.
4. W1: I need to buy a pencil. It costs a quarter.
   W2: A pencil is a quarter? I'll buy one, too.
5. M1: How much is coffee? I only have a one-dollar bill.
   W1: That's OK. Coffee is one dollar.

6. M2: I have a five-dollar bill. Is that enough for the book?
   W2: Yes, the book is five dollars.
7. W1: The gas bill is forty-five dollars this month. Please write a check.
   M1: I have the check right here.
8. M1: We need a money order for the rent.
   W2: I have a money order for $300 right here.

Pg. 77 Lesson 1—Exercise 2B

W = Woman, N = Narrator
1. W: There are many customers in the store. One customer is waiting in line.
   N: customer
2. W: The cashier takes money and gives change. It's important to give correct change.
   N: change
3. W: The lady in line is buying a dress. It's a blue dress.
   N: dress
4. W: She is also buying some shoes. The shoes are on the counter.
   N: shoes
5. W: There are some socks next to the shoes. The socks are on sale.
   N: socks
6. W: That man with the bag is wearing a suit. It's a brown suit.
   N: suit
7. W: Men's shirts are on sale. For only $19.99, you can buy this shirt.
   N: shirt
8. W: Ties are on sale, too. Do you need a tie?
   N: tie
9. W: The salesperson is wearing a blouse. Her blouse is yellow.
   N: blouse
10. W: The salesperson is also wearing a skirt. She usually wears a skirt to work.
    N: skirt
11. W: The salesperson is helping a young man in a T-shirt. He's wearing a red T-shirt.
    N: T-shirt
12. W: The young man is also wearing gray pants. He might buy some new pants today.
    N: pants

Pg. 79 Lesson 2—Exercise 3A

J = John
J: My name is John. These are the clothes I like to wear. At home, I usually wear a T-shirt and jeans. I also wear my favorite sneakers. At work, I wear a hat, a uniform, and a belt. On special occasions, I like to look good. I wear my favorite suit, tie, and shoes. How about you? What clothes do you like to wear?

Pg. 83 Lesson 4—Exercise 1E

M = Man Customer, S = Salesperson, W = Woman Customer
1. M: Excuse me. Is this jacket a large? I need a large.
   S: Yes, it is. It's eighty dollars.
   M: Did you say eighteen or eighty?
   S: It's eighty dollars.
   M: OK, thanks. I'll think about it.
2. S: Can I help you with something?
   W: Yes. This blouse and this skirt are beautiful. What size are they?
   S: They're both small.
   W: Are they on sale?
   S: Yes, they are. The blouse is seventeen dollars and the skirt is only sixteen dollars.
   W: Great! I'll take them both in small.
3. M: Excuse me. I need a medium jacket and a medium T-shirt.
   S: These are medium.
   M: How much are they?
   S: The jacket is nineteen ninety-nine and the T-shirts are on sale for five dollars each.

Pg. 83 Lesson 4—Exercise 2C

M = Man, W = Woman
1. M: How much are the shoes?
   W: They're fifty dollars.
2. W: How much is the shirt?
   M: It's sixteen dollars.
3. W: That's one dress and one sweater. Your total is forty twenty-eight.
4. M: OK. Here you go. Your change is twelve sixty.
5. W: That tie is on sale. It's ten eighteen.
6. M: Thank you very much. Your change is six dollars and ninety cents.

UNIT 8   Eating Well

Pg. 88 Lesson 1—Exercise 1B

M1 = Man 1, M2 = Man 2, W1 = Woman 1, W2 = Woman 2
1. W1: I need to buy fruit.
   M1: Fruit? We have a special on bananas.
2. M1: What vegetables are fresh today?
   W1: Vegetables? We have fresh lettuce and carrots.
3. M1: The man in the white shirt is carrying a basket.
   W1: The basket is blue.
4. M1: The red shopping cart is outside.
   W1: A woman is pushing the cart.
5. M1: What is the checker doing?
   M2: The checker is ringing up the food.
6. W1: The young man is the bagger.
   W2: The bagger is putting the food in bags.

Pg. 89 Lesson 1—Exercise 2B

W = Woman, N = Narrator
1. W: I go to the supermarket every week. This week, I'm buying bananas. Everyone in my family eats bananas.
   N: bananas

2. W: These apples look delicious. I always put apples in the kids' lunches.
   N: apples
3. W: Lettuce is on sale this week. I can make a salad with lettuce for dinner.
   N: lettuce
4. W: Milk is expensive this week, but my kids drink milk every day.
   N: milk
5. W: I'm buying a dozen eggs. There's a sale on eggs this week.
   N: eggs
6. W: Look at these beautiful red tomatoes. My husband loves tomatoes.
   N: tomatoes
7. W: I buy bread every week. My kids like white bread.
   N: bread
8. W: This is my favorite soup. I like to have soup for lunch.
   N: soup
9. W: I'm making chicken for dinner tonight. My whole family likes chicken.
   N: chicken
10. W: These are nice sweet onions. My son loves onions.
    N: onions
11. W: I buy grapes when they are on sale. Grapes are a healthy snack.
    N: grapes
12. W: I'm also buying potatoes. Tomorrow, we'll have potatoes with dinner.
    N: potatoes

Pg. 91 Lesson 2—Exercise 3B

M = Mr. Garcia, MS = Mrs. Garcia
MS: OK, let's see what's on sale this week. Ground beef is $1.89 a pound. That's great. We need ground beef. Peanut butter is $3.99. No, that's too expensive. We need tuna fish and carrots. We don't need beans and we don't need spaghetti this week. Oh, that's my favorite cheese! It's $2.10 a pound. It's on sale this week. I can have a little cheese. Ramon? Do you need anything special from the supermarket?
M: Well, don't forget my oranges.
MS: OK, oranges.

Pg. 95 Lesson 4—Exercise 1E

P1 = Pizza Store Employee 1, P2 = Pizza Store Employee 2, P3 = Pizza Store Employee 3, C1 = Woman Customer 1, C2 = Man Customer, C3 = Woman Customer 2
1. P1: Are you ready to order?
   C1: Yes, I am. I'd like two large pizzas with onions and one small pizza with pepperoni.
   P1: Anything to drink?
   C1: Yes, please. I'd like two small sodas.
   P1: That's two large pizzas with onions, one small pizza with pepperoni, and two small sodas.
   C1: Yes, that's right.

2. P2: Are you ready to order?
   C2: Yes, I'm ready. I'd like one medium pizza with peppers.
   P2: That's one medium pizza with peppers. Anything to drink?
   C2: Yes. Two large iced teas and one medium soda.
   P2: One medium pizza with peppers, two large iced teas, and one medium soda coming up.
3. P3: Are you ready to order?
   C3: Yes, I'm ready. I'd like two small pizzas with onions and mushrooms.
   P3: OK, anything to drink?
   C3: Yes, please. I'd like one small soda and two large iced teas.
   P3: That's two small pizzas with onions and mushrooms, one small soda, and two large iced teas.
   C3: That's right. Thank you.

Pg. 95 Lesson 4—Exercise 2B

M = Man, W = Woman
1. M: I'd like a large pizza.
2. W: Do you want anything to drink?
3. M: Are you ready to order?
4. W: I never eat lunch at home.

UNIT 9 Your Health

Pg. 100 Lesson 1—Exercise 1B

R = Receptionist, W1 = Woman 1, W2 = Woman 2, W3 = Woman 3, M1 = Man 1, M2 = Man 2, M3 = Man 3
1. R: Doctor's office. How can I help you today?
   W1: This is Ming Lee calling. My head hurts.
2. R: Doctor's office. How can I help you today?
   M1: Hello. This is Miguel Diaz. I hurt my nose.
   R: I'm sorry to hear that.
   M1: Yes. I got hit in the nose with a baseball. It really hurts!
3. R: Hello, Ms. Singh. I understand that you need to see the doctor.
   W2: Yes. My neck hurts.
4. R: Is there anything else?
   W2: Yes. My back hurts, too.
5. R: Doctor's office. Can I help you?
   M2: This is Raji Patel. My chest hurts.
   R: Mr. Patel, do you need an ambulance?
   M2: No, it's not that bad. I just want to see the doctor.
6. R: Doctor's office? Can I help you?
   M3: Yes. This is Niles Gold. I have to see the doctor about my arm. My arm hurts.
7. R: Does anything else hurt?
   M3: Yes, my hand hurts, too.
8. R: So, Ms. Vega, do you need to see the doctor this week?
   W3: Yes I do. My foot hurts.
9. R: OK, Ms. Vega. The doctor can see you tomorrow at 11 a.m. Is there anything else?
   W3: Yes, my leg hurts, too.

Pg. 101 Lesson 1—Exercise 2B

M = Man, N = Narrator, N1 = Nurse
1. M: Hi. My name is Michael. I'm at the doctor's office. It's very busy at the doctor's office today.
   N: doctor's office
2. M: I'm sick. I have a stomachache. It's no fun having a stomachache.
   N: stomachache
3. M: The lady next to me has an earache. She says she gets bad earaches twice a month.
   N: earache
4. M: I think the girl over there has a fever. Her face is hot and red. It's probably a fever.
   N: fever
5. M: The woman at the receptionist's window has a cold. I hope I don't get her cold!
   N: cold
6. M: The receptionist is talking to the woman with a cold. The receptionist is working hard today.
   N: receptionist
7. M: In fact, I think she has a headache. She has her hand on her head. Yes, I'm sure she has a headache.
   N: headache
8. M: The lady next to me, the girl over there, and I are all patients today. There are other patients here, too.
   N: patients
9. M: The man in the center of the room has a backache. It's terrible to have a backache.
   N: backache
10. M: Wow! That soccer player has a broken leg. I know from experience. It's no fun to have a broken leg.
    N: broken leg
11. M: The doctor is giving the man a prescription for some medicine. That's Doctor Kim. She's a great doctor.
    N: doctor
12. M: There's the nurse. She has a chart. I think she's looking for me.
    N1: Michael? Michael Chen?
    M: Excuse me, the nurse is calling me.
    N: nurse

Pg. 103 Lesson 2—Exercise 3B

D = Doctor, M1 = Man 1, M2 = Man 2, M3 = Man 3, M4 = Man 4, W1 = Woman 1, W2 = Woman 2
1. D: What's the matter today Mr. Jones?
   M1: Well, Dr. Moss, I don't feel well. I have a stomachache.
   D: When did it start?
   M1: Yesterday.
   D: Tell me about your diet, Mr. Jones.
   M1: I don't eat lunch. I drink a lot of soda and coffee.
   D: Mr. Jones, you have to change your diet.
2. D: How are you today, Mrs. Lynn?
   W1: Not so good. I have a terrible headache.
   D: Take this medicine.
   W1: Thanks, Doctor.

3. D: What seems to be the problem, Mr. Martinez?
   M2: Oh, Doctor Moss, I have a bad cold.
   D: Say "Ahhhh."
   M2: "Ahhhhhhhhhhhhhhhhhhhhhh."
   D: Yes, you have a cold. Drink a lot of fluids. Try hot tea or juice.
   M2: OK, Dr. Moss. Achoo!
   D: Bless you.
4. W2: I don't feel well. I sit at my desk and I'm tired all day, Dr. Moss.
   D: Ms. Mendoza, you have to exercise three or four times a week.
5. M3: I have a terrible backache today, Dr. Moss.
   D: You have to stay home and rest for forty-eight hours, Mr. White.
6. D: I'm worried about your blood pressure, Mr. Wang. You have to quit smoking.
   M4: Yes, Dr. Moss. I know.

Pg. 107 Lesson 4—Exercise 1E

MR = Man Receptionist, WR = Woman Receptionist, M1 = Man 1, M2 = Man 2
1. MR: Good morning. Dr. Wu's Dental Clinic.
   M1: This is Tom Garcia. I have to make an appointment with the dentist.
   MR: OK. The first opening I have is on Tuesday, June 2nd at 4:00 in the afternoon. Is that OK?
   M1: 4:00 on Tuesday? Yes, that's fine.
   MR: OK, Tom. We'll see you at 4:00 on Tuesday, June 2nd.
2. WR: Dr. Brown's office. Can I help you?
   M2: Yes, this is Pat McGee. I have to see Dr. Brown for an eye examination.
   WR: OK, Pat. I have an appointment available on October 23rd at 10:30 a.m. Is that OK?
   M2: October 23rd? Yes, that's a Monday. That's fine.
   WR: OK, then. Thanks, Pat. See you on Monday, October 23rd at 10:30.

Pg. 107 Lesson 4—Exercise 3C

M = Man, W = Woman
1. W: What does he have to do today?
2. M: She has to work at 9:00.
3. W: Who has a new car?
4. M: We have two children.

UNIT 10 Getting the Job

Pg. 112 Lesson 1—Exercise 1B

M1 = Man 1, M2 = Man 2, M3 = Man 3, W1 = Woman 1, W2 = Woman 2, W3 = Woman 3
1. M1: I work at the pharmacy. I fill prescriptions. I like my job because I help people feel better. I'm a pharmacist.
2. W1: I work in my home. I take care of my family and our home. It's a lot of work, but I love my family. I'm a homemaker.
3. M2: I work in a garage. I fix a lot of cars. My friends love my job because I fix their cars, too. I'm a mechanic.

4. M3: I work at a school. I keep the school buildings clean. I'm a janitor.
5. W2: I work at Fran's Fancy Restaurant. I am a server. I am the best server in the restaurant.
6. W3: I work at a day care center. I take care of children all day. I love my job. I'm a childcare worker.

Pg. 113 Lesson 1—Exercise 2B

M1 = Man 1, N = Narrator, M2 = Man 2, M3 = Man 3, M4 = Man 4, M5 = Man 5, M6 = Man 6, W1 = Woman 1, W2 = Woman 2

1. M1: Hi. I'm Lars. I'm delivering food to the restaurant. I'm a delivery person.
   N: delivery person
2. W1: I'm Young Hee. Today is a very big day for me. I manage the restaurant. I'm the manager.
   N: manager
3. W2: I'm Nancy. Today is my first day. I serve food to the customers. I'm a server.
   N: server
4. M2: Hi. I'm Henry. I clean the tables and help Nancy. I'm the bus person.
   N: bus person
5. M3: Hello. I'm Tomas. I can't talk now. I'm busy. I have to cook the food. I'm the cook.
   N: cook
6. M4: I'm Pat. I'm fixing the sink now. I'm the plumber.
   N: plumber
7. M5: I'm Oliver. I'm painting the building for the big grand opening. I'm the painter.
   N: painter
8. M6: I'm Nate. I plant flowers. These are going to be beautiful. I'm a gardener.
   N: gardener

Pg. 119 Lesson 4—Exercise 1E

M1 = Man 1, M2 = Man 2, W1 = Woman 1, W2 = Woman 2, W3 = Woman 3

1. W1: My name is Gladys. I lived in El Salvador for twenty years. I was a full-time nurse. I can help patients.
2. M1: My name is Ken. I lived in Japan and studied English. I was a pharmacist. I can fill prescriptions.
3. M2: My name is Franco. I was a plumber in Mexico for many years. I can fix sinks and toilets.
4. W3: My name is Molly. I studied business and stayed home with my children for five years. I can cook, clean, pay bills, and take care of children.

Pg. 119 Lesson 4—Exercise 3B

M = Man, W = Woman

1. W: I can't fix the sink.
2. M: I can plant flowers.
3. W: I can take care of children.
4. M: I can't fill prescriptions.
5. W: I can't speak Spanish.
6. M: I can cook Mexican food.

UNIT 11 Safety First

Pg. 124 Lesson 1—Exercise 1B

M = Man, W = Woman

1. M: Be careful. There's a stop sign. You have to stop and look for other cars at a stop sign.
2. W: Be careful. That's a road work sign. You have to watch for people working on the street when you see a road work sign.
3. W: Look out! There's a school crossing sign. You have to slow down and look for children at a school crossing sign.
4. M: Don't park there. There's a "no parking" sign. You can't park next to a "no parking" sign. You have to park somewhere else.
5. W: The sign says "no left turn." You can't turn left. You can only turn right.
6. M: Slow down! The speed limit sign says "35." You have to pay attention to the speed limit sign.

Pg. 125 Lesson 1—Exercise 2B

W = Woman, N = Narrator

1. W: There's an emergency exit on the left. The emergency exit is always open during the workday.
   N: emergency exit
2. W: Ann and Joe are factory workers. These factory workers come to work at 7:30 a.m.
   N: factory workers
3. W: Joe is wearing his hard hat. He knows that a hard hat will keep his head safe.
   N: hard hat
4. W: Joe is also wearing safety glasses. He always wears his safety glasses at work.
   N: safety glasses
5. W: Joe is also wearing his safety gloves. Sometimes he works with chemicals. He always wears safety gloves then.
   N: safety gloves
6. W: Joe is wearing his safety boots, too. He wears his safety boots every day.
   N: safety boots
7. W: This warehouse is a safe workplace. A safe workplace is important for everybody.
   N: safe
8. W: There's a fire extinguisher on the wall. All the workers learn to use the fire extinguisher.
   N: fire extinguisher
9. W: Tanya is very careful at work. She pays attention and wears her safety equipment. She's a careful worker.
   N: careful
10. W: This warehouse is dangerous, or unsafe. It's important to pay attention to dangerous situations and things.
    N: dangerous, unsafe
11. W: Tim is careless at work. He never pays attention and he doesn't wear safety equipment. He's a careless worker.
    N: careless

12. W: Look out, Tim! The floor is wet! Tim doesn't see
       the wet floor.
    N: wet floor

Page 127 Lesson 2—Exercise 3A

NA = News Anchor
NA: Good evening. This is Leticia Gomez at Channel
       13 News with tonight's special edition: Are you
       safe on the road, at work, and at home? Take the
       following quiz to find out.
1. Do you always drive the speed limit?
2. Do you drive fast near school crossings?
3. Do you know where the emergency exits are in the
   building?
4. Do you wear safety equipment at work?
5. Do you have a smoke detector in the kitchen?
   Remember to be safe. This is Leticia Gomez reporting.
   Good night.

Pg. 131 Lesson 4—Exercise 1E

M1 = Man 1, M2 = Man 2, M3 = Man 3, W1 = Woman 1,
W2 = Woman 2, W3 = Woman 3
1. M1: 911. What's the emergency?
   W1: A car accident on my street.
   M1: Where is the accident?
   W1: On the corner of Pine Avenue and Hope Street.
   M1: Is anyone hurt?
   W1: Yes, a man.
   M1: OK. Help is on the way.
2. W2: 911. What's the emergency?
   M2: There's a robbery.
   W2: What's the address?
   M2: 3310 Main Street.
   W2: Is anyone hurt?
   M2: Yes, the manager.
   W2: OK, sir. A police officer is on the way.
3. W2: 911. What's your emergency?
   W3: There's a fire in the house across the street.
   W2: What's the address?
   W3: It's 615 Elm Street.
   W2: Is anyone hurt?
   W3: Yes, a young woman.
   W2: OK, I'll send an ambulance.
4. W2: 911. What's your emergency?
   M3: There's been a bad car accident.
   W2: Where's the accident?
   M3: It's on 1st Street.
   W2: Is anyone hurt?
   M3: Yes. Two men are hurt.

Pg. 131 Lesson 4—Exercise 2A

M = Mother, B = Boy, D = Daughter, F = Father
M: You should eat your vegetables.
B: Why? Why should I eat vegetables?
M: You should eat vegetables because they're good for you.
M: You shouldn't smoke.
D: I know I shouldn't. I shouldn't smoke because it's bad
   for me. Don't worry, Mom. I know.
M: You should wash the car.
F: I know I should. The car is dirty. I should wash it today.
M: You're right. You should wash it and I should help you.

Pg. 131 Lesson 4—Exercise 2B

M = Man, W = Woman
1. W: You shouldn't park there.
2. M: For a healthy diet, you should eat these.
3. W: At work, you should do this.
4. M: When you have a cold, you shouldn't do this.
5. M: When you are driving, you should do this.
6. W: At home, you shouldn't do this.

UNIT 12 Free Time

Pg. 136 Lesson 1—Exercise 1B

WM = Weatherman
1. WM: Hello and Happy New Year! It's snowing this
       New Year's. It's going to keep snowing all day.
2. WM: Yes, it's raining this Presidents' Day, so don't
       forget your umbrella. It's raining hard.
3. WM: It's a little cloudy this Mother's Day. It's cloudy,
       but there's no rain. Go ahead and take Mom to
       the park for some fun.
4. WM: Hello, and Happy Father's Day. It's a beautiful
       sunny day today, so go out and enjoy the
       sunny weather with Dad.
5. WM: It's hot this Independence Day. It's hot at the
       park. It's hot at the beach. Wherever you go,
       drink lots of water and have a great 4th of July.
6. WM: Happy Thanksgiving, everyone. Brrrr! It sure is
       cold out. I'm going to get out of the cold and
       have some turkey with my family. Enjoy your
       holiday, everybody.

Pg. 137 Lesson 1—Exercise 2B

W = Woman, N = Narrator
1. W: In the winter, the weather is very cold in our city.
      We like to stay home. On snowy days, we stay
      home and relax together.
   N: stay home
2. W: When we have enough snow, the kids make a
      snowman. My son is outside making a snowman
      now.
   N: make a snowman
3. W: In the spring, the weather is usually nice. We like
      to go to the park and have a picnic. My daughter
      and I are getting ready to have a picnic now.
   N: have a picnic
4. W: My husband and my son love to play soccer.
      They are playing soccer now.
   N: play soccer
5. W: It's hot in our city in the summer. We like to go
      to the beach. In the summer, we go to the beach
      every weekend.
   N: go to the beach
6. W: There's a boy swimming in the ocean. On a hot
      summer day, it's great to go swimming.
   N: go swimming
7. W: The weather changes a lot in the fall here.
      Sometimes it's sunny. Sometimes it's cloudy and
      windy. When it's nice, we like to go out to eat.
      We go out to eat once or twice a month.
   N: go out to eat

8. W: We also like to go to the movies in the fall. Look. Some people across the street are going to go to the movies.
   N: go to the movies

Pg. 139 Lesson 2—Exercise 3A

M = Man, W = Woman

1. W: I'm taking the number one bus. What's the first stop?
   M: The number one bus stops at Grant Street at 8:00 a.m.
2. M: What time does the number two bus stop at the school?
   W: It stops at Front Street School at 12:15.
3. W: I work at the mall. I have to be there at 9:00.
   M: You can take the number one bus. It stops at the mall at 8:30.
4. W: I'm taking my children to the baseball game. It starts at 5:00. What time does the number three bus stop at the baseball stadium?
   M: The number three bus stops at the Riverside Baseball Stadium at 4:45.
   W: Great!
5. W: Let's go to the park today for lunch. What time does the number two bus stop there?
   M: The number two stops at the park at 1:00. That's a good time for lunch!

Pg. 142 Lesson 4—Exercise 1E

N = Norma, G = Gloria

G: Hi, Norma.
N: Hi, Gloria. What are you doing?
G: I'm going to see a movie. Do you want to go with me?
N: Sure. What are you going to see?
G: I want to see *Rain in My Eyes*. It's a love story. It's playing at 9:30.
N: *Rain in My Eyes*? That sounds good. Let's go then.
G: OK. If we go at 9:30, and it's over by 11:30 we can take the last bus.
N: That's great! I'll meet you at the bus stop at 9:00.
G: OK. Bye.

Pg. 143 Lesson 4—Exercise 2B

M = Man, W = Woman

1. M: I'm going to go to the market.
2. W: I wanna eat dinner at 6:00.
3. M: I want to study at the library tomorrow.
4. W: I'm gonna call my mother this evening.
5. M: Do you wanna go to the beach with us tomorrow?

THE SIMPLE PRESENT WITH *BE*

Statements

I	am	
You	are	a student.
He She	is	
It	is	a book.
We You They	are	students.

Negative statements

I	am not	
You	are not	a student.
He She	is not	
It	is not	a book.
We You They	are not	students.

Contractions

I am = I'm	I am not = I'm not
you are = you're	you are not = you're not / you aren't
he is = he's	he is not = he's not / he isn't
she is = she's	she is not = she's not / she isn't
it is = it's	it is not = it's not / it isn't
we are = we're	we are not = we're not / we aren't
they are = they're	they are not = they're not / they aren't

Yes/No questions

Am	I	
Are	you	
Is	he she it	happy?
Are	we you they	

Answers

Yes,	I	am.
	you	are.
	he she it	is.
	we you they	are.

No,	I	am not.
	you	aren't.
	he she it	isn't.
	we you they	aren't.

Information questions

Where	am	I?
How	are	you?
Who	is	he? she?
When	is	it?
Where What	are	we? you? they?

THE PRESENT CONTINUOUS

Statements

I	am	
You	are	
He She It	is	sleeping.
We You They	are	

Negative statements

I	am not	
You	aren't	
He She It	isn't	sleeping.
We You They	aren't	

Yes/No questions

Am	I	
Are	you	
Is	he she it	eating?
Are	we you they	

Answers

Yes,	I	am.
	you	are.
	he she it	is.
	we you they	are.

No,	I	am not.
	you	aren't.
	he she it	isn't.
	we you they	aren't.

Information questions

Where	am	I	going?
When	are	you	
Who Why	is	he she	calling?
How	is	it	working?
What	are	we you they	doing?

THE SIMPLE PRESENT

Statements

I You	work.
He She It	works.
We You They	work.

Negative statements

I You	don't	
He She It	doesn't	work.
We You They	don't	

Contractions

do not = don't
does not = doesn't

Yes/No questions

Do	I you	
Does	he she it	work?
Do	we you they	

Answers

Yes,	I you	do.	No,	I you	don't.
	he she it	does.		he she it	doesn't.
	we you they	do.		we you they	don't.

Information questions

What	do	I you	study?
Who	does	he she	see?
How	does	it	work?
Where When Why	do	we you they	work?

THE SIMPLE PAST WITH *BE*

Statements

I	was	
You	were	
He She It	was	here.
We You They	were	

Negative statements

I	wasn't	
You	weren't	
He She It	wasn't	here.
We You They	weren't	

Contractions

was not = wasn't
were not = weren't

Yes/No questions

Was	I	
Were	you	
Was	he she it	late?
Were	we you they	

Answers

Yes,	I	was.	No,	I	wasn't.
	you	were.		you	weren't.
	he she it	was.		he she it	wasn't.
	we you they	were.		we you they	weren't.

Information questions

Where	was	I	yesterday?
Why	were	you	in Texas?
Who	was	he? she?	
What	was	it?	
When	were	we	here?
How	were	you they	yesterday?

THE FUTURE WITH *BE GOING TO*

Statements

I	am		
You	are	going to	have a party tomorrow.
He She	is		
It	is	going to	rain in two days.
We You They	are	going to	visit friends next week.

Negative statements

I	am not		
You	aren't	going to	have a party tomorrow.
He She	isn't		
It	isn't	going to	rain in two days.
We You They	aren't	going to	visit friends next week.

Yes/No questions

Am	I		
Are	you	going to	work?
Is	he she		
Is	it	going to	snow?
Are	we you they	going to	go?

Answers

Yes,	I	am.	No,	I	am not.		
	you	are.		you	aren't.		
	he she it	is.		he she it	isn't.		
	we you they	are.		we you they	aren't.		

Information questions

Who	am	I	going to	see?
	are	you		
When What	is	he she it	going to	eat?
How Why What	are	we you they	going to	study?

CAN AND *SHOULD*

Statements

I You He She It We You They	can should	work.

Negative statements

I You He She It We You They	can't shouldn't	work.

Contractions

cannot = can't
should not = shouldn't

Yes/No questions

Can Should	I you he she it we you they	work?

Answers

Yes,	I you he she it we you they	can. should.	No,	I you he she it we you they	can't. shouldn't.	

Information questions

Who What	can should	I you	see?
When Why How	can should	he she it	help?
Where	can should	we you they	travel?

THERE IS/THERE ARE

Statements		
There	is	a pencil.
	are	pencils.

Negative statements		
There	isn't	a pencil.
	aren't	pencils.

Yes/No questions		
Is	there	a pencil.
Are		pens?

Answers						
Yes,	there	is.	No,	there	isn't.
		are.			aren't.

Questions with How many			
How many	pens	are	there?

Answers		
There	is	one pen.
	are	two pens.

THIS, THAT, THESE, AND THOSE

Singular statements		Notes
This That	sofa is new.	Use *this* and *these* when the people or things are near.
This That	is new.	

Plural statements		Notes
These Those	sofas are new.	Use *that* and *those* when the people or things are far.
These Those	are new.	

Yes/No questions
Is that sofa new?

Answers
Yes, it is.

Yes/No questions
Are these sofas new?

Answers
Yes, they are.

A, AN, ANY, AND SOME

Singular questions	
Do you have	a tomato? an onion?

Answers
Yes, I have an onion.
No, I don't have an onion.

Plural questions		
Do you have	any	tomatoes? onions?

Answers
Yes, I have some tomatoes.
No, I don't have any tomatoes.

NOUNS

To make plural nouns	Examples	
For most nouns, add -s.	chair—chairs	office—offices
If nouns end in -s, -z, -sh, -ch, -x, add -es.	bus—buses	lunch—lunches
If nouns end in consonant + -y, change -y to -ies.	family—families	factory—factories
If nouns end in vowel + -y, keep -y.	boy—boys	day—days
For most nouns that end in -o, add -s.	photo—photos	radio—radios
For some nouns that end in -o, add -es.	tomato—tomatoes	potato—potatoes
For most nouns that end in -f or -fe, change -f or -fe to v. Add -es.	wife—wives	half—halves
Some plural nouns do not end in -s, -es, or -ies. They are irregular plurals.	child—children	person—people

PRONOUNS AND POSSESSIVE ADJECTIVES

Subject pronouns	Object pronouns	Possessive adjectives
I	me	my
you	you	your
he	him	his
she	her	her
it	it	its
we	us	our
you	you	your
they	them	their

POSSESSIVES

Singular nouns		Notes
Tom's The manager's The factory's The woman's The person's	office is big.	Use -'s after a name, person, or thing for the possessive. Tom's the factory's

Plural regular nouns		Notes
The managers' The factories'	offices are big.	For plural nouns, change -s to -s'. the managers'

Plural irregular nouns		Notes
The women's The people's	office is big.	For irregular plurals, add -'s. women's

Information questions			
What color is	my your Tom's Sara's the cat's our your their	hair?	

Answers	
My Your His Her Its Our Your Their	hair is black.

PREPOSITIONS

Times and dates		Notes
The party is	on Tuesday. on June 16th.	Use *on* for days and dates.
The party is	at 9:30. at 9 o'clock.	Use *at* for times.

Locations		
The bank is	next to behind in front of across from	the library.
The bank is	between	the library and the store.

FREQUENCY AND TIME EXPRESSIONS

Frequency expressions			
I You	exercise		
He She It	exercises	every once a twice a three times a	day. week. month. year.
We You They	exercise		

Adverbs of frequency		
I You		exercise.
He She It	always usually sometimes never	exercises.
We You They		exercise.

Questions and answers with *How often*	
A: How often do they exercise? B: They exercise every month.	A: How often does she exercise? B: She always exercises.
A: How often does he exercise? B: He exercises once a day.	A: How often do you exercise? B: I never exercise.

STATEMENTS WITH *AND, BUT, OR*

Notes	Examples
To combine sentences, use *and*. Change the first period to a comma.	I need a quarter. Amy wants a dime. I need a quarter, and Amy wants a dime.
For sentences with different ideas, use *but*. Change the first period to a comma.	I have a nickel. I don't have a quarter. I have nickel, but I don't have a quarter.
To combine two options, use *or*. Change the first period to a comma.	I want 10¢. I need a dime. I need ten pennies. I want 10¢. I need a dime, or I need ten pennies.

VOCABULARY LIST

A

accident	60
address	6
adult	36
aisle	88
alone	128
angry	20
answer the phone	66
apartment building	54
apple	89
apply for a job	114
appointment	106
area code	6
arm	100
ask	12
ATM card	84
attractive	31
aunt	29
average	31

B

back	100
backache	101
bagger	88
banana	89
bank	52
baseball game	138
basket	88
bathroom	40
bathtub	41
bed	41
bedroom	40
bicycle	53
billion	144
birthday	34
black	18
blocks	58
blond	30
blood pressure	102
blouse	77
blue	18
board	5
book	5
bookcase	41
boss	120
boy	30
bread	89
breakfast	64
broken	101
brother	29
brown	18
brush teeth	68
bus	53
bus person	113

bus stop	53
business	113
business owner	116
buy	90

C

call	48
can	119
car	53
careful	125
careless	125
carrots	91
cart	88
cash	78
cell phone	126
chair	5
change	77
change your diet	103
check (noun)	76
check (verb)	126
checker	88
checkup	108
chest	100
chicken	89
child	28
childcare center	112
childcare worker	112
children	28
Christmas	144
classmate	8
classroom	8
clean	44
clinic	54
clock	5
close	4
cloudy	136
cold (noun)	101
cold (adj.)	136
color	18
come home	64
computer	9
cook	113
cook dinner	42
cookies	90
copy	71
copy machine	66
corner	58
country	24
cousin	29
co-worker	120
credit card	78
customer	77
cut the grass	42

D

daily routine	72
dangerous	125
date	17
date of birth	18
daughter	28
day	17
deliver packages	113
delivery person	113
dentist	104
desk	5
dictionary	5
difficult	38
dime	76
dining area	40
do homework	65
do housework	65
doctor	101
doctor's office	101
door	9
dress	77
dresser	41
drink	65
drink fluids	103
drive	103
driver	132
dust	44

E

earache	101
easy	38
eat	44
egg	89
electric	46
email address	6
emergency	60
emergency exit	125
emergency kit	60
employee	120
evening	10
exactly	108
exercise	68
exit map	60
expensive	48
experience	118
extra large	82
eyes	30

F

factory workers	125
fall	137
family	30
farmer	116
fast	126

father	28
Father's Day	136
favorite	18
fee	84
feel better	108
fever	101
fill	70
fill in	22
fire	60
fire extinguisher	125
fire station	52
first name	6
fish	90
five-dollar bill	76
fix	113
follow directions	108
food	113
foot	100
form	6
free time	72
fruit	88
full-time	115

G

garage	40
gardener	113
gas	46
gas station	53
get dressed	64
get ready	72
get up	64
girl	30
go	12
go out to eat	137
go swimming	137
go to bed	64
go to the beach	137
go to the movies	137
goodbye	10
grandfather	29
grandmother	29
grandparents	29
grandson	29
grapes	89
gray	18
green	18
greeting card	144
group	8

H

hair	30
hand	100
happy	20
hard hat	125

have	80
have a picnic	137
have lunch	65
have to	104
head	100
headache	101
healthy	96
heavy	31
help	12
help-wanted ad	114
holiday	136
homemaker	112
hospital	52
hot	136
hour	72
hungry	20
hurt	100
husband	28

I

ice cream	90
iced tea	94
Independence Day	136
insurance card	102
Internet	114
interview	114

J

jacket	80
janitor	112
job	66

K

| kitchen | 40 |

L

label	97
large	36
last name	6
law	132
leave the house	68
left	58
leg	100
letter	4
lettuce	89
library	54
like	66
listen to	4
listen to music	42
live	18
living room	40
lock	128
long distance	48
look for	90

| look for a job | 114 |

M

make	60
make a snowman	137
make dinner	64
mall	78
man	30
manage	113
manager	67
married	22
mechanic	112
medicine	102
medium	82
meet	60
midnight	16
miles	59
milk	89
million	24
money order	76
month	17
mop	44
morning	10
mother	28
Mother's Day	136
mouth	102
movie theater	53
mushroom	94

N

name	6
neck	100
need	80
neighborhood	54
neighbors	60
new	38
New Year's Day	136
newspaper	114
nickel	76
no left turn	124
no parking	124
noon	16
nose	100
notebook	5
nurse	101
nutritionist	96

O

occasion	144
office	66
old	38
on sale	78
one-dollar bill	76
onion	89

open (verb)	4
open (adj.)	128
orange	18
oranges	90
order	92
over-the-counter medicine	108

P

paint	113
painter	113
pants	77
parents	28
park	54
parking lot	53
partner	8
part-time	115
patient	101
pay	46
pay attention	132
pay period	121
pen	5
pencil	9
penny	76
people	24
pepperoni	94
peppers	94
percent	36
pharmacist	112
pharmacy	53
phone	46
phone book	145
pick up	104
pink	18
pizza	92
play a video game	42
play soccer	137
plumber	113
point to	4
police station	52
population	24
post office	54
potato	89
power outage	60
prepare	60
prescription	102
Presidents' Day	136
price	78
print	6
printer	70
proud	20
pull over	132
purple	18
push a button	70

Q

quarter	76
quit smoking	103

R

rain	136
rate of pay	121
read	12
read a map	132
receipt	84
receptionist	101
red	18
refrigerator	41
relax	66
rent	76
repeat	4
rest	102
restaurant	53
ride	53
right	58
road work	124
rug	41

S

safe	125
safety boots	125
safety equipment	125
safety glasses	125
safety gloves	125
salt	97
save	48
say	4
schedule	66
school	12
school crossing	124
seat belt	126
serve	113
server	112
shirt	77
shoes	77
shop	78
shopping list	90
short	30
should	126
sick	102
sign (verb)	6
sign (noun)	124
single	22
sink	41
sister	29
sit down	4
size	82
skirt	77

sleep	42
small	36
smoke detector	126
snow	136
socks	77
soda	95
sofa	41
son	28
sore throat	102
soup	89
speak	12
special occasion	79
speed limit	124
spell	6
spend time	72
spring	137
stand up	4
staple	71
stapler	70
stay home	102
stomachache	101
stop	124
stop sign	53
stove	41
straight	58
student	5
study	12
suit	77
summer	137
sunny	136
supermarket	52
sweater	78

T

table	41
take a shower	48
talk	47
talk to	115
tall	30
tan	18
teacher	5
telephone number	6
tell	6
temperature	102
Thanksgiving	136
thin	31
tickets	142
tie	77
time	17
time card	121
tired	20
today	17
tomato	89
tomorrow	17

toothache	104
T-shirt	77
turn	58
turn off	70
turn off lights	48
turn on	66
TV (television)	41

U

uncle	29
unhealthy	96
unsafe	125
usually	78
utility bill	46

V

vacuum	44
Valentine's Day	144
vegetable	88

W

walk	65
want	80
warning	109
wash	44
watch TV	42
water	46
wear	79
week	17
weekend	69
wet floor	125
white	18
wife	28
window	9
winter	137
withdraw	84
woman	31
work	65
worried	20
write	22

X, Y, Z

year	17
yellow	18
yesterday	17
young	31

INDEX

ACADEMIC SKILLS

Grammar

A little and *a lot,* 72, 73
Adverbs of frequency, 98, 126
A or *an,* 29, 38
And, too, and *but,* 122
A, some, and *any,* 86
Be
    Contractions, 9–11, 14, 15
    Information questions, 19, 23, 26, 27
    Negative statements, 8, 9
    Or questions, 23
    Simple past, 116, 117, 122, 123
    Statements, 9–11, 14, 15, 116, 117, 122, 123
    Yes/No questions, 20, 21, 23, 117, 122, 146
Can
    Questions and statements, 119, 122
Frequency expressions, 92, 93, 98, 99
Future with *be going to*
    Contractions, 140, 141, 146, 147
    Information questions, 141, 146, 147
    Negative statements, 140
    Statements, 140, 141, 143, 146, 147
Have, 74, 80, 81, 86, 87
Have to, 104, 105, 107, 110, 111
    Information questions, 105, 107, 110, 111
How much/How many, 62, 63, 77, 82
How often, 93, 98, 99
Irregular plural nouns, 110
Need, 80–83, 86, 87
Possessive adjectives, 32, 33, 38, 39
    Information questions, 33, 38, 39
Possessive nouns, 33
Prepositions
    of location, 54, 55, 58, 59, 62, 63
    on or *at,* 107, 110
Present continuous
    Contractions, 44
    Information questions, 45, 50
    Negative statements, 44, 50
    Statements, 44, 45, 47, 50
    Yes/No questions, 50
Should and *should not*
    Information questions with *should,* 129
    Negative statements, 128, 129, 131, 134 ,135
        Contractions, 128
    Statements, 128, 129, 131, 134, 135
    Yes/No questions with *should,* 134
Simple past
    Simple past with *be,* 116, 117, 122, 123
    Yes/No questions with *be,* 117, 122, 146
Simple present
    Contractions, 68
    Negative statements, 68, 74
    Yes/No questions, 80, 81, 86, 87
    Statements, 68, 69, 74, 75
Singular and plural nouns, 5, 14
Subject and object pronouns, 47
There is and *There are*
    Negative statements, 56, 57, 62, 63
    Statements, 56, 57, 62, 63
    Yes/No questions, 57, 62, 63
This and *that,* 43
Want, 80–83, 86, 87
What, 14
Who, 14

Graphs, Charts, Maps

24, 25, 37, 52, 55, 58, 59, 61, 73, 133, 144

Listening

Activities in the home, 42
Asking for help, 46
ATM machine, using, 84, 87
Bus schedule, 139
Classroom directions, 4, 5
Clothing, 77, 79, 82, 83
    Clothing sizes and prices, 77, 82, 83
Colors, 40
Conserving resources, 48
Daily routines, 64–66, 71, 72
Directions, 54–59
Doctor's appointments, 102, 106, 107
Emergencies, 60, 130
Food, 89, 91, 96, 97
Food labels, 97
Food shopping, 88–91
Forms, 6, 23
Getting well, 103
Greeting cards, 144
Holidays, 136
ID cards, 19
Identifying currency, 76
Illnesses and injuries, 101
Information questions, 19, 22, 23
Instructions, 70
Leisure activities, 137, 138
Meeting people, 10, 11, 15
Modes of transportation, 53
Money, 76, 77
Movies, 142
Neighborhood maps and places, 52–59
Numbers, 34, 35, 83
Obligations, 111
Parts of the body, 100, 102
Paying bills, 46
Personal information, 6, 7
Physical descriptions, 30–33
Places and things in the home, 41, 42, 43
Plans, 147
Pronunciation, 11, 35, 59, 71, 83, 95, 107, 119, 131, 143
Relaxation, 67, 72
Responsibilities, 64–67, 72
Restaurant, ordering food, 94, 95
Road safety, 124, 133
Safety checklist, 127
Safety precautions, 126

Shopping at the mall, 78
Studying English, 12
Talking about a classroom, 5
Telephone messages, 35
Time, 16
Utility bills, 46–49
Weather, 136
Weekend plans, 138
Work safety, 125
Work schedule, 66

Math

Addition, 47, 59, 73, 95, 143
Calculating amounts of change, 83
Calculating bill totals, 47, 95
Calculating distances, 59
Calculating pay, 121
Calculating times, 143
Division, 127
Multiplication, 121
Percentages, 36, 37, 127
Population statistics, 25
Subtraction, 35, 83

Problem Solving

Analyzing and negotiating, 99
Appropriate behavior after an accident, 135
Comparing jobs, 123
Correcting errors on documents, 39
Delegating responsibilities, 51
Determining what to do when lost, 63
Handling obligations when sick, 111
Modifying plans due to bad weather, 147
Resolving ATM problems, 39
Responding to greetings and introductions, 15
Solving problems in the workplace, 75
Solving problems with forms, 27

Pronunciation

Can/can't, 119
Contractions, 11
Ending sounds, 71
Formal and relaxed, 143
Have to/has to, 107
Intonation patterns, 95
Numbers, 35, 83
Should/shouldn't, 131
Stressed words in sentences, 59

Reading

Activities in the home, 42
Addressing envelopes, 49
ATM cards, 84, 85
Checks, 85
Clothing, 82
Countries and populations, 24, 25
Daily routines in the U.S., 72, 73
Doctor's appointment, 102
Emergency exit maps, 61

Employee behavior, ideal, 120, 121
Family size, 36, 37
Food labels, 97
Food shopping, 90
Getting a job, 114, 115
Good health, 108, 109
Greeting cards, 144, 145
Healthy food, 96, 97
Help-wanted ads, 115
Home emergencies, 60, 61
Housework, 73
Medicine labels, 109
Neighborhoods, 54, 56
Phone books, 145
Safe and dangerous behavior, 126
Safe driving, 132, 133
Saving money, 48, 49
School forms, 6
Shopping at a mall, 78
Study habits, 12, 13
Time cards, 121
Traffic accidents, 133
Weekend plans, 138
Work schedules, 66

Speaking

Activities in the home, 44, 45, 51
Birthdays, 34, 35
Bus schedule, 139
Calendar, 17
Classrooms, 5, 8, 9, 15, 56
Clothing, 77, 79, 82, 83
Daily routines, 68, 69, 71–73, 75
Describing family members, 29
Describing people, 31–33, 39
Directions, 55, 58, 59
Doctor's appointments, 106, 107
Emergencies, 130, 131
Employment, 113, 115, 119, 123
Food shopping, 91, 93
Food, 91
Getting well, 103
Home emergencies, 60, 61
Housework, 73
Illnesses and injuries, 101
Interpersonal information, 18, 19, 21, 25, 27
Job interviews, 118
Leisure activities, 137
Medicine labels, 109
Menu prices, 94
Money, 76, 77, 83
Movie times and prices, 143
Neighborhood places, 53, 57, 63
Numbers, 35, 83
Obligations, 105, 107, 111
Office machines and equipment, 70, 71
Paying bills, 46, 49, 51
Personal information, 7, 11, 15
Phone books, 145

Plans, 139, 141, 147
Preventive care, 108, 109
Prices, 77, 82, 83
Restaurant, ordering food, 94, 95
Road safety, 125,132
Safety checklist, 127
Schedules, 65, 67
Shopping and money, 85
Talking about clothes, 79–81, 87
Things in the home, 41, 43
Time, 17
Utility bills, 46, 48, 49
Work safety, 125, 136

Writing

Addressing envelopes, 49
Calendar words, 17, 27
Classroom directions, 5
Classrooms, 9, 15
Clothing, 77, 81
Daily routines, 65, 68, 69, 71–73, 75
Describing people, 30–33, 38, 39
Doctor's appointments, 102, 107
Employment, 112–117, 123
Food, 91
Food labels, 97
Food shopping, 91, 93
Giving advice, 147
Illnesses and injuries, 111
Interpersonal information, 18, 21, 25, 27
Leisure Activities, 137, 139
Medicine labels, 109
Menu prices, 94
Money, 76, 77, 83
Neighborhood places, 52, 53, 55–57, 59, 62, 63
Numbers, 35, 46, 47, 83
Obligations, 105, 107, 111
Office machines and equipment, 70
Parts of the body, 100, 101
Places and activities in the home, 40, 43, 45, 51
Plans, 139, 141, 147
Restaurant, ordering food, 95
Road safety, 125, 135
Safe and unsafe behavior, 126, 127
Safety equipment, 125
Schedules, 67, 69
Shopping, 79
Things in the home, 43, 51
Time cards, 121
Transportation, 53
Utility bills, 46, 48, 49

CIVICS

Directory (Locate maps and services), 52–55, 58, 59, 61
Diversity, 18, 19, 21, 24–27
DMV, 124, 125, 127, 132–135
Emergencies, 130–132, 134

Employment requirements, 112, 113, 116–119, 122
Employment resources, 114, 115, 123
Employment safety, 125, 127, 135
Health care, 101–103, 106–110
Health—emergencies, 129–131, 134
Locating community resources, 46, 49, 145
Nutrition, 96, 97, 99
Pharmacy, 109
Recreation, 137–143, 147
Safety measures, 124–129, 132, 133, 135

LIFE SKILLS

Consumer Education

ATMs and banking, 84, 85
Clothing, 77, 79, 82, 83
Counting and using currency, 76, 77, 83
Identifying clothing, 77–79
Restaurant menus, 94, 95
Selecting clothing, 82
Utility bills, 46–49

Environment and the World

Maps, 59
Weather, 136, 137, 146, 147

Family and Parenting

Family members, 28–30, 32, 33, 38, 39
Family size, 36, 37
Holidays, 136

Government and Community Resources

Addresses, 6, 7, 49

Health and Nutrition

Body parts, 100, 101
Common illnesses and injuries, 101, 102
Directions and warnings on medicine labels, 109
Getting well and staying healthy, 103, 108
Healthy foods, 96, 97
Making a doctor's appointment, 106

Interpersonal Communication

Information about classmates, 25
Introductions, 10, 11, 15
Leisure activities, 137, 138, 142
Making plans, 139, 141, 147
Personal information, 7, 18
Personal interviews, 21, 27

Safety and Security

Emergencies, 130, 131
Home emergencies, 60, 61
Road safety, 125–127, 132, 135
Safe and dangerous behaviors, 126, 127
Safety checklists, 127
Work safety, 125, 135

Telephone

Bills, 46, 48, 49
Listening to movie times, 142
Messages, taking, 35
Requesting information, 139
Telephone numbers, 6, 7
Using a phone book, 145

Time and Money

Calendar, 17, 34, 35, 38
Checks, 85
Clock time, 16, 17
Ordinal and cardinal numbers, 35, 49, 83
Paying bills, 46–49
Time cards, 121
Time, 16
U.S. coins and currency, 76, 77, 83

Transportation and Travel

Bus schedules, 139
Road safety, 125–127, 132, 135

TOPICS

At Home, 40–51
Daily Routines, 64–75
Eating Well, 88–99
Family and Friends, 28–39
The First Step, 2–3
Free Time, 136–147
Getting the Job, 112–123
In the Classroom, 4–15
In the Neighborhood, 52–63
My Classmates, 16–27
Safety First, 124–135
Shop and Spend, 76–87
Your Health, 100–111

WORKFORCE SKILLS

Applied Technology

Using office machines and equipment, 70, 75

Maintaining Employment

Workplace expectations, 120
Work-related vocabulary, 113, 116–121

Obtaining Employment

Applying for a job, 115, 118
Help-wanted ads, 114, 115, 123
Job interviews, 118
Job skills, 113, 116–119

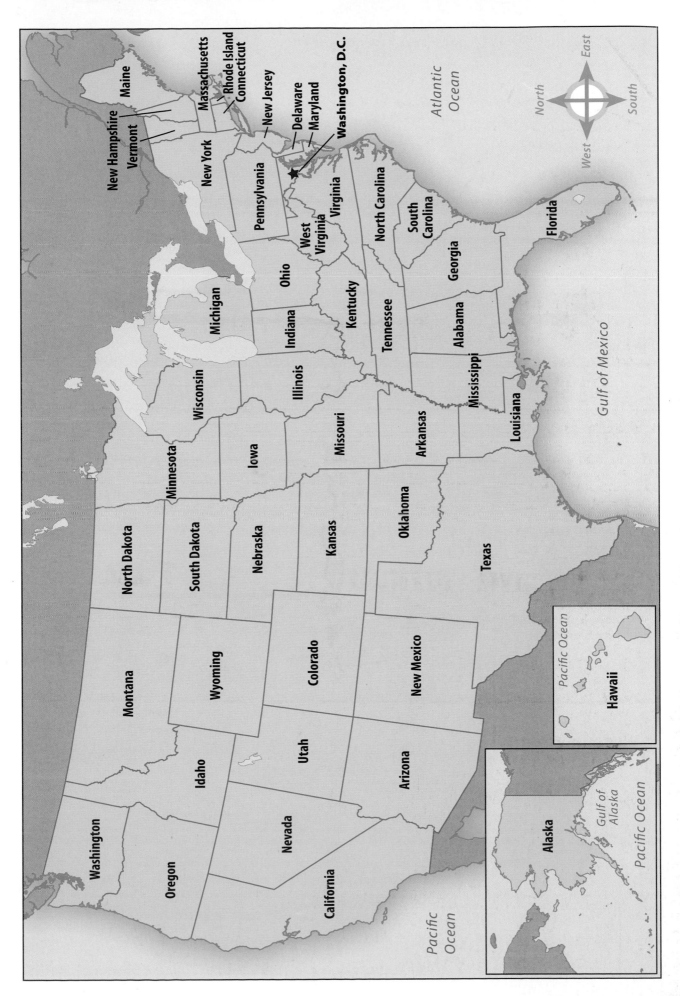